D1476804

EGraphointer

# TONLE SAP
## The Heart of Cambodia's Natural Heritage

# TONLE SAP

## The Heart of Cambodia's Natural Heritage

Colin Poole

Photographs by Eleanor Briggs

RIVER
BOOKS

First edition published in Thailand in 2005 by
River Books Co., Ltd.
396 Maharaj Road, Tatien, Bangkok 10200
Tel: 66 2 6221900, 2254963, 2246686
Fax: 66 2 2253861
E-mail: paisarn@riverbooksbk.com
www.riverbooksbk.com

ISBN: 974 9863 15 1

Publisher: Narisa Chakrabongse
Design: Holger Jacobs, Helena Dietrich
at Mind Design, London
Production Supervision: Paisarn Piammattawat

Printed and bound in Thailand
by Sirivatana Printing Co., Ltd.

COVER:
**Fishermen and bamboo fishing
lot fence, fishing lot #2,
Battambang**

BACK COVER:
**Collecting grass from the last
natural flooded wetland of the
Mekong Delta, Boeng Prek
Lapeou, Takeo**

TITLE PAGE:
**An aerial view of a lone
fisherman on the Tonle Sap
floodplain**

THIS PAGE:
**Breeding Darters in the Prek
Toal Core Area of the Tonle Sap
Biosphere Reserve**

# CONTENTS

# FOREWORD

Tonle Sap, the largest freshwater lake in Southeast Asia, has been referred to as its heart', with a rhythm defined by the ebb and flow of the Mekong River, pumping natural resources into the region, and supporting a plethora of wild species. The first time I saw it, I was with Eleanor Briggs and Colin Poole, who through this book will introduce the vital ecosystem to even more audiences. Colin was directing WCS's country program, and Eleanor was the tireless advocate and supporter of Cambodian conservation.

In May 2002, the water was down, with the Mekong not yet swollen by the monsoon rains. A still morning, with the lake reflecting the sky-blue-pink, lines of fishing boats, and the swirling of foraging birds: lines of moving Asian Openbills and Painted Storks, Adjutants, squadrons of Spot-billed Pelicans herding fish, and against the sky in their breeding trees, colonies of Darters. Maintaining the biological productivity of the lake must remain a high priority, not only to conserve these globally important waterbird species, but because Tonle Sap is the source of much of the animal protein in Cambodia, and directly sustains the livelihoods of over a million people in and around the lake.

The threats to that productivity include interruptions to the flow of water on the Mekong by dam building; local overexploitation of wildlife, especially fish, reptiles and birds; and the deterioration of traditional management regimes, some of which go back 1,200 years. It is people who will address these threats – people like those at Prek Toal who depend directly on the lake, people in the national government and civil society who recognize the centrality of Tonle Sap to the very survival of the country, and people in the global community, in organizations like WCS, who are impressed by its global importance. Knowing about something is key to doing something about it, and this book is a powerful contribution to that knowledge.

*Dr John G. Robinson*
Senior Vice-President and Director of International Conservation, Wildlife Conservation Society

*This book was supported by the Wildlife Conservation Society. WCS works globally in 57 countries to save wildlife and wildlands by understanding and resolving critical problems that threaten key species and large, wild ecosystems around the world. WCS believes in the intrinsic value of the diversity and integrity of life on Earth and in the importance of wildlife and wilderness to the quality of human life.*

WCS,
2300 Southern Boulevard,
Bronx, NY 10460, USA
www.wcs.org

Composite Radarsat image of the Tonle Sap at the height of the flood in 2000 showing the extent of inundation of the floodplain.
Image used courtesy of the Mekong River Commission

# DEDICATION

This book is dedicated to the late Sam Veasna, friend, colleague and inspiration to both of us. His early death at the age of 33 was great loss for wildlife conservation in Cambodia.

Veasna was head of the Provincial Wildlife Officer in Siem Reap and died tragically in early December 1999 from cerebral malaria contracted during fieldwork searching for Kouprey in Anlong Veng. He was a single-handed force for conservation in northern Cambodia and during his tragically short life achieved more than most will do in a lifetime. Without him, the conservation area for Sarus Cranes at Ang Trapeang Thmor would never been declared. It was his work and lobbying that provided the basis for the designation, and one of his last tasks was to draw up the initial boundaries for the reserve.

Veasna's passion for wildlife now lives on in the Sam Veasna Centre for Wildlife Conservation. Built with funds raised from friends and colleagues around the world, the centre promotes an interest in local wildlife conservation for both locals and foreigners alike. Situated in central Siem Reap, along the road from the Angkor Village Hotel, it welcomes visitors.

**Sam Veasna in 1999 using the first Cambodian language bird book to talk to villagers about conservation in the village of Pong Ro, adjacent to Ang Trapeang Thmor, Banteay Meanchey**

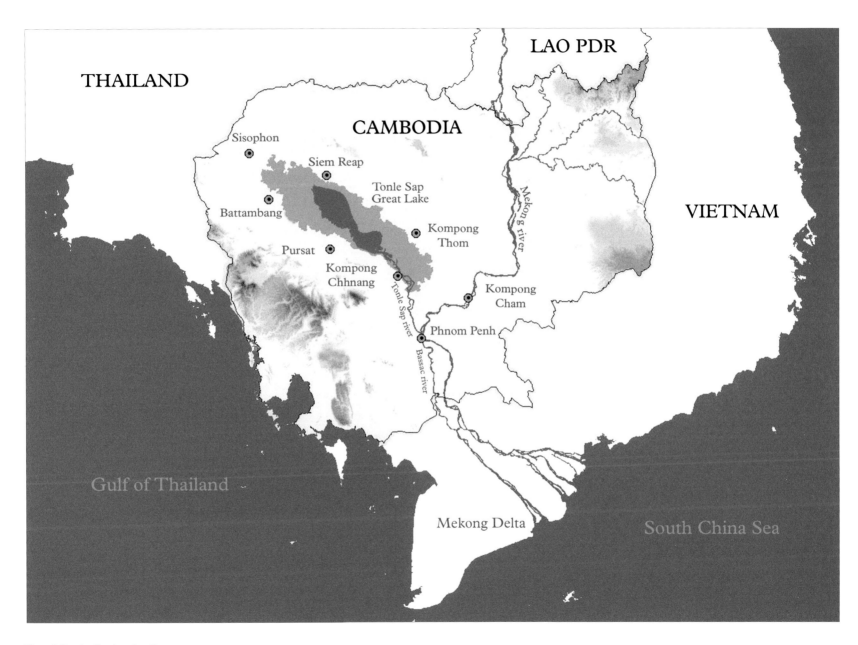

**Map of Cambodia showing the
Tonle Sap and major towns**

# PHNOM KULEN: MOUNTAIN AND FOREST

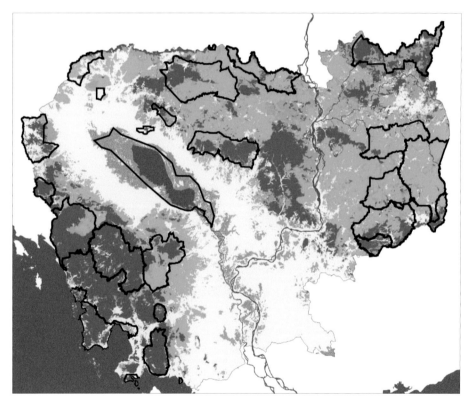

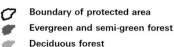
◻ Boundary of protected area
▪ Evergreen and semi-green forest
▪ Deciduous forest

**Map of Cambodia showing the extent of forest areas
and the boundaries of all the different protected areas**

Hidden amongst the foliage at a high point on the south-east side of the Kulen plateau is a three-tiered laterite structure, around 100 metres square and 10 metres high. Unassuming today, this structure, known as Rong Chen, was built for a ceremony in 802 that would inaugurate the foundation of one of the world's greatest empires. It marks the beginning of modern day Cambodia and the point that still remains, more than 1,200 years later, its spiritual birthplace.

The highest part of Phnom (Mount) Kulen rises to around 500 metres above the northern plains. Thirty kilometres north-east of Siem Reap it is the closest range of hills to the Tonle Sap, and Phnom Kulen is Cambodia's most sacred mountain. Over centuries it has provided not only the water that keeps Siem Reap fed throughout the dry season, but sandstone from which many of the great temples of Angkor were hewn, wood that built countless houses and palaces, animals and birds that filled stomachs and medicinal markets throughout the region, and perfumes that ended up as far away as China and the Middle East.

The mythical status of Kulen began with King Jayavarman II. Hinduism had already arrived with travelling merchants and priests, and Jayavarman II saw Kulen, or as it was then Mahendraparvata, as symbolising the cosmological centre of the Hindu universe. In his eyes, Kulen dominated the Tonle Sap floodplain in the same way that Mount Meru rose above the mythical oceans. It was therefore on the summit of Kulen – where the earth met the heavens and men met gods – that he was ordained. Here in 802, in an elaborate ceremony at Rong

The well forested foothills that remain surrounding the plateau of Phnom Kulen

The river of 1000 *lingas* flowing off the forested Kulen plateau at Kbal Spean

Washing with the holy water of the Siem Reap River after it rises from Phnom Kulen

Chen, presided over by a Brahmin priest, Jayavarman II became the self-appointed intermediary between men and gods. He was crowned "the God who is King" and the first Emperor of Kambujadesa – Cambodia.

Today the most stunning parts of Kulen that remains are the carvings that adorn the rocks of the river beds. These are believed to have been created during the 11th century, long after the consecration ceremony, and probably primarily during the period of King Udayadityavarman II between1050-1066. Two tributaries of the Siem Reap River are known to have been decorated in this manner, one rising from the east of the plateau, and the other 10km west along the range at Kbal Spean. The carvings at Kbal Spean, some of the most beautiful, weren't discovered by modern archaeologists until 1968, and perhaps more remain yet to be discovered on remote forested streams around Kulen.

The Hindu ceremony of *abishek* – the cleansing of sacred figures through ritual bathing – infuses them with spiritual energy or *shakti*. On Kulen, by carving these sacred images into the riverbed, the ancient Khmers were using the rivers to perform *abishek* on a giant scale. They ensured that not only were the figures constantly bathed, but the water passing over them became charged with spiritual energy. The most prolific carvings are the large number of Shiva *lingas*, leading to the name "river of a thousand *lingas*". As the water flows over these *lingas* it is endowed with the creative force of Shiva, the Hindu lord of the universe.

In the river and on its banks are also images of a creation myth involving Vishnu. He is represented in

RIGHT:
**Patterns of hundreds of *lingas* on the stream bed at Kbal Spean**

BELOW:
**An abstract of a single *linga* carved within several concentric *yonis***

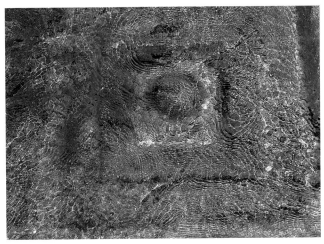

eternal sleep reclining on the back of a naga – the serpent Ananta. As they float upon the waters of the cosmic ocean, with his consort Lakshmi at his feet, Vishnu dreams the universe into existence and Brahma is born on a lotus blooming from his navel. The dreaming Vishnu's first creation is the water of the oceans of consciousness, so placing these carved images at the source of the river ensured the continuous creation of blessed water. To the ancient Hindu Khmer the Siem Reap River was their Ganges. As long as the river flowed from the holy mountain, the continual bathing of gods and images of creation provided the Angkorian civilisation below with everlasting health and fertility.

The ancient link between kingship and Kulen continues as today the mountain is again "protected" by the monarchy. In 1993 King Norodom Sihanouk signed a Royal Decree designating 23 protected areas, one of which was the Phnom Kulen National Park. The park is officially managed by the Ministry of Environment with a small number of rangers employed to guard its resources. However they face an uphill battle. Although Kulen is still forested in comparison to the lands around it, trees once stretched unchallenged in all directions from the summit to the lakeshore. The continued loss of forest plagues modern day Cambodia and sadly for Kulen the power of kingship is not what it once was, and neither its sacred status nor royal patronage has saved the mountain from such pillage.

The modern story of Kulen is unfortunately the story of most of Cambodia's protected areas. Having been set up with much foreign encouragement and assistance

ABOVE:
**Reclining Vishnu with Lakshmi at his feet and Brahma on a lotus blooming from his navel, Kbal Spean**

FAR LEFT:
***Lingas* surrounding another reclining Vishnu, Kbal Spean. The head of Lakshmi at his feet has been stolen by looters.**

Monks crossing the Siem Reap
River on Phnom Kulen

under the then new Ministry of Environment, neither the Government nor the donor community ever provided the level of political or financial support to enable them to succeed. On paper they may meet the criteria of the World Conservation Union (IUCN), but on the ground reality is very different. Boundaries for most areas have never been legally demarcated, and many of the communities living within them still have no knowledge of the land's "protected" status or what that may mean.

The real tragedy for many of these areas is that their designation may have resulted in them receiving less protection and increased the rates of degradation. In most protected areas, resource exploitation, particularly logging and hunting, has been rife. So much so, that in the late 1990s when teams of Cambodian and foreign scientists carried out the country's first detailed biodiversity surveys, the results were surprising. They often found better forest and healthier wildlife populations in logging concessions than in adjacent protected areas. The reason was simple, in sharp contrast to the Ministry of Environment, timber barons had the financial and political muscle necessary to protect their investment.

Over the past ten years the environmental NGO Global Witness has been recording and publicising instances of forest crime in Cambodia. Inside the Phnom Kulen National Park they have documented multiple cases of timber cutting and the construction of illegal roads. They have even produced evidence to link some of these activities directly to members of the Cambodian military[1]. Unfortunately this is far from unusual, as across the country Global Witness has shown the Royal Cambodian Armed Forces to be the country's largest commercial timber extractors. Many licensed forest concessionaires sub-contracted their logging to the military. In a country still experiencing post-conflict recovery, with an oversized and underpaid army, perhaps it is not surprising that soldiers turn to the free market and increased exploitation of their natural resources to make a living?

Whether motivated by poverty or greed, at what cost to the future has been the continued large scale stripping of forest resources? Many issues have been linked to deforestation in Cambodia; increasing floods, temperatures, soil erosion and siltation to name but a few. However, with the lack of any form of long-term – or even short-term – data it is difficult to confirm or deny any of these, or isolate them from wider global issues. What is certain is that Cambodia still has extensive natural forest cover,

far greater than its neighbours Thailand and Vietnam, but much of what is of value within that forest, both in economic and biodiversity terms, has been lost. Patterns of forest cover and the nature of the forest resources are changing, and therefore so is the ancient relationship between people and forests.

Cambodia has a long history of forest exploitation, it is said that life starts with a wood cradle, then a wooden house, and at its close a wooden coffin and cubic metre of firewood for the cremation[2]. The people of Angkor lived in wood houses, and even the Kings' palaces were constructed from timber. Stone was only used for temples and other religious constructions, as they were built to honour gods and therefore had also to be immortal. In contrast the wood used for housing needed not to exceed the lives

OPPOSITE:
**Phnong resin-tapper in Mondulkiri about to extinguish a fire he has lit inside the tree to stimulate the production of resin**

LEFT:
**Moving timber by ox-cart along the main street of Kompong Phluk, Siem Reap, in the dry season**

BELOW:
**Cut logs lying in a timber yard, Anlong Veng**

of men and has long since disappeared. All that remains to be seen today are the wood sockets in the stone work. It is the now treeless lands between Angkor and Kulen that would have provided much of this timber.

Timber is not all that was taken from the forest. A whole range of other products have long been collected, used and sold. Although almost completely gone from the forests around Kulen, aquilaria wood has long been harvested from trees throughout the country. Aquilaria is a fragrant fungal infection that only grows inside particular trees. It has been used for centuries to make expensive perfumes, particularly in the Middle East.

Another tree product sometimes used in perfume production, and still collected in the area today, is resin from dipterocarp trees. These trees are immediately noticeable by the large burnt holes near the base of the trunk. Every week a fire is lit in the hole and the tree exudes a sticky, almost tar-like, liquid resin. This is collected and then sold, primarily for sealing wooden boats, but also as a base for perfumes. Current research indicates that long term use of such trees for resin may well be sustainable and perhaps will never actually kill the tree[3]. The real threat comes from logging, as the four key resin bearing trees happen also to be some of the most valuable timber species.

Wildlife has also been trapped and traded for centuries. Reliefs of the Bayon and Angkor depict bird hunters, and animal parts such as rhinoceros horn and elephant ivory were said to be sold to China. Even through the Khmer Rouge period of the late 1970s, when the country was almost shut off to the outside world, wildlife was still being traded. The historian Ben Kiernan has documented shipments of forest products destined for China during the Democratic Kampuchea regime that included extraordinary amounts of wildlife[4]. One in March 1977 included 18 tons of deer horns and seven tons of pangolin scales. Another in May 1977 included over six tons of monkey bones, 1.5 tons of elephant bones and "24,670 pieces" – apparently individual animals – of dried geckos, weighing over half a ton. Into September 1978, a shipment included 49 tiger skins and 29 leopard skins. Other shipments of forest products left for North Korea at the same time.

Today wildlife hunting and trade continues, and represents one of the greatest current threats to the coutry's rich natural heritage. Even within the Phnom Kulen National Park wildlife is openly for sale. On the summit of the mountain, along side the small children selling t-shirts, bamboo flutes and coca-cola, are stalls selling dried skins of lorises (a small nocturnal primate), teeth of bears and cats, feet of Serow (a goat-like ungulate) and muntjacs and many other bizarre animal parts. Wildlife hunting and trade takes many forms, and whilst the export of wildlife, much ultimately still ending up in China, continues in huge quantities, what happens at Kulen is different.

There is a long Khmer tradition of assigning medicinal and magical values to specific animal parts, one that is significantly different from other regional cultures. Comparisons with traditional Chinese medicine and its use of wildlife show few, if any, similarities. In Cambodia, animals such as lorises are treasured for the properties of their skin. The skin is dried and sold in small pieces to be soaked in wine; when drunk this is said to provide various therapeutic properties. Such use of animals has never been formally studied, but is intimately linked to mythology and magic, with many of the parts possessing specific spiritual properties. Kulen's status as a sacred mountain not only provides special powers to the river, but also the forest and to the animals and birds that live there. The tooth of a bear from Kulen is more potent than one from elsewhere, and therefore in greater demand and consequently more expensive.

What effect this has had on the wildlife of Kulen is undocumented. However, what little is known, along with evidence from similar areas, indicates that Kulen is now an "empty forest". Wildlife populations on the range are severely depleted and the larger mammals, such as Asian Elephants and Tigers, have already been hunted out. Unfortunately, following such local extinctions the problem is no longer just confined to the immediate area. A look at what's for sale in the market reveals parts of animals such as bears and Serow which will have already been lost from the range. Now Kulen's sacred status is driving a trade in wildlife parts from other areas. Animals are being hunted elsewhere and their parts transported to Kulen to be sold at a premium price under the guise that they came from the mountain itself.

As Cambodia enters a time of peace following decades of war and insecurity, such trade is increasingly possible as roads are built and land mines cleared, allowing access to previously remote or unsafe areas of the country. This is essential for development and the lifting of rural people out of poverty. However, along with the increased access has come a wave of immigration and land

ABOVE LEFT:
**Examining muntjac antlers for sale at a traditional medicine stall on Phnom Kulen**

ABOVE:
**A dried loris skin for sale for traditional medicine on Phnom Kulen**

claims. To drive regularly along any new rural highway in a forested area is to witness the gradual destruction of all the forest, often for kilometres around. Invariably the process of clearing and claiming land involves first burning everything. At the height of the dry season the smoking, desecrated landscape conjures up Hollywood images of post-nuclear holocaust.

In many areas productive ground is being turned to wasteland as no crops are planted, or if they are, sterile monoculture plantations are created, destined, without proper care, never to fulfil their potential. Increasingly popular in many parts of the country are cashew plantations, but these too present many risks and problems. Introduced from South America the tree produces a chemical that is toxic to most other plants, consequently not only is a cashew plantation a true monocultured 'desert', but the soil remains poisoned – apparently inhibiting any natural regeneration or other crop growth for years to come. Cashew farmers also rely upon a global market with a known pattern of boom and bust. It may be profitable now, but what when the market crashes? Many people, especially those on the land, will not have the security previously provided by crop diversity, nor the financial reserves to prevent entering another cycle of poverty and debt.

As much of the valuable timber has already been removed, the greatest threat is now no longer logging but clearing forest for land speculation. As the forest concession system becomes increasingly unviable due to the decreasing value of the remaining standing timber, land is instead being sold off or grabbed, much for large-scale

agricultural or land concessions. The result is that land remains in the hands of the wealthy and those dependent upon the remaining forest resources are denied access.

Around Siem Reap these issues are particularly acute due to the high land value. As tourism grows and the town booms, land grabbing is increasing, not only in the immediate vicinity of Angkor, but gradually throughout the province, further and further away from the town itself [5]. Without sensible and effective land-use planning, how many years will it be before the remaining areas of forest 50 or even 100 kilometres from Siem Reap are converted into country resorts, theme parks or golf courses? At least that appears to be what a lot of speculators are banking on. With the new land law the government has the tools to involve local people in making decisions on the land on which they live. It now remains to be seen how effectively it can be used.

One final twist is that while many rural people throughout the country utilise forest resources, their real dependence upon them is little understood. A recent study has in fact demonstrated that even for communities living within the forest, their primary, and preferred, source of protein is not what comes from the forest, but what comes from the water. They are reliant upon the fish from the streams. The effect of the changing nature and patterns of forest resources on these stream fisheries is unknown and is a topic in need of urgent further investigation, but it is unlikely to be positive. It is the riches of the water rather than those of the forest on which people are truly dependent.

Perhaps therefore the true centre of Cambodia, spiritually and culturally, is not Phnom Kulen, but the Siem Reap River? Cambodia's Ganges rather than its Mount Meru? It is in the water that the true source of life is to be found at so many different levels. In every village people's lives are shaped by their relationship with water, its annual fluctuations and the riches it brings. It is a story that is repeated again and again in every community on the long journey downriver to the Mekong delta, and one that will be retold in different ways throughout this book.

Cast-net fishing in a forest
stream, Mondulkiri

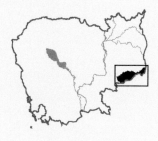

In the province of Mondulkiri, along the border with Vietnam, stands the most biologically diverse area of hill evergreen and semi-evergreen forest left in the country. It is home to eight species of primate, more birds than anywhere else in the country and is the only area thus far where automatic 'camera-traps' have proved a population of tigers remain. In addition it is home for the Phnong, an ethnic group who live within the evergreen forest and represent Cambodia's only truly forest dependent community.

Originally a forest concession, its resources were well

**A Government team patrolling the Seima Biodiversity Conservation Area, Mondulkiri**

protected by the foreign investor who bought the rights to harvest the area. Through the recent process of national forest reform and with the changing climate of forestry investment, the concessionaire has now withdrawn from the area, and the Ministry of Agriculture, Forestry and Fisheries has designated it the Seima Biodiversity Conservation Area. With support from the Wildlife Conservation Society and a number of international donors, the government's Forestry Administration is now managing a core of 140,000 hectares of evergreen and semi-evergreen forest for conservation.

The greatest threat to the integrity of the area comes not from those living within it, but from outsiders coming to log, clear land, hunt or electro-fish. The management regime is working with the indigenous Phnong to protect the area and conserve the key components of biodiversity by both minimising the negative impacts of the outside influences, and assisting the Phnong to formalise their legal rights to the area. Phnong livelihoods are dependent not on hunting, but primarily on resin-tapping, shifting agriculture and fishing forest streams. Their prime protein source is not terrestrial wildlife but fish. As such, in this remote area of Cambodia, a new partnership for forest conservation has been born.

The initiative involves four key components. The first is government ranger patrol teams to enforce forest laws against hunting and logging; the second is working with the local Phnong communities on livelihood issues; the third mapping patterns of land and resource use for community titling and zoning, and the fourth a biological monitoring program looking at both populations of wildlife and key forest resources.

Early indications are that things are working. In the face of clearance for kilometres around the forest is still secure, and populations of wildlife are holding steady and even increasing. In fact an early morning trip up the old logging road from Keo Seima to the provincial capital Sen Monorom is probably the easiest way in Cambodia to see globally threatened animals such as Douc Langur, Yellow-cheeked Gibbon and Green Peafowl feeding along the edge of the highway. Endangered wildlife happy to show itself, safe in the knowledge any people are unlikely to be hunters with guns.

# ANGKOR: THE ANCIENT ENVIRONMENT

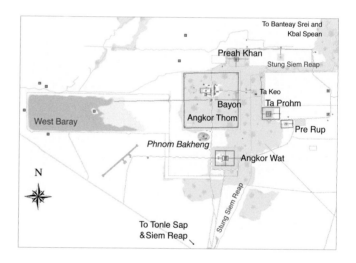

Today the Angkor World Heritage site is an oasis, containing approximately 40 square kilometres of the only remaining lowland, old-growth forest in Siem Reap. As such it is almost as much a relict of Cambodia's natural heritage as of its cultural past. During the day Pied Hornbills, pigeons and vast flocks of parakeets feed among the large fruit trees, while every night flying-foxes leave their roost in front of Siem Reap's Royal Palace to fly and feast in the same trees. Turtles still inhabit the moats and Long-tailed Macaques the forest around many of the temples – although increasingly now they rob tourists rather than forage on wild fruit.

What we see today is but a fragment of what once existed. Fortunately it is not difficult to recreate what it must have been like, as the ancient Khmers have left us in the carved bas-reliefs on the temple walls, beautifully accurate 'photographs' of their environment. Perhaps the most important and beautiful of these are found around the Bayon, particularly the depictions of everyday life in the southern gallery. Here, among scenes of battle, the natural environment is just as intricately illustrated by artists with first-hand experience of the habitats and animals. Plants, mammals, birds, reptiles and fish are often identifiable to family level and sometimes to a particular species.

Fish are by far the most commonly-depicted creature on Angkorian reliefs, and although nobody has ever counted them all, there must be thousands. In one famous scene alone 'The Churning of the Ocean of Milk', found in the eastern gallery of Angkor Wat, there are well over 1,000 individual fish representations. A thematic approach to studying the fish bas-reliefs of Angkor was recently undertaken by icthyologist Tyson Roberts[6]. He discovered that the great majority of the fish can only be identified to family level, but distinguished nine distinct families and hypothesised on several specific identifications. Most common is the carp, which is the dominant family in the Mekong Basin. Although he found the execution of the images varied greatly, in some cases it was so accurate that he suggested the sculptors or artists worked from actual fish specimens.

Roberts confirmed that the key fish bas-reliefs on the Bayon and Angkor Wat are not of marine life as is sometimes proposed, but are based on the fish of the Mekong Basin. All the identifiable fish come primarily from local freshwater groups and are species that die on exposure to

LEFT:
**Fishing bird, perhaps cormorant or darter, bas relief, Bayon Temple**

BELOW LEFT:
**Monkeys in the trees, Bayon south gallery**

**Deer and birds, bas relief, Bayon Temple south gallery**

Dancing cranes beneath fish,
turtles and crocodiles, bas
relief, Bayon Temple south
gallery

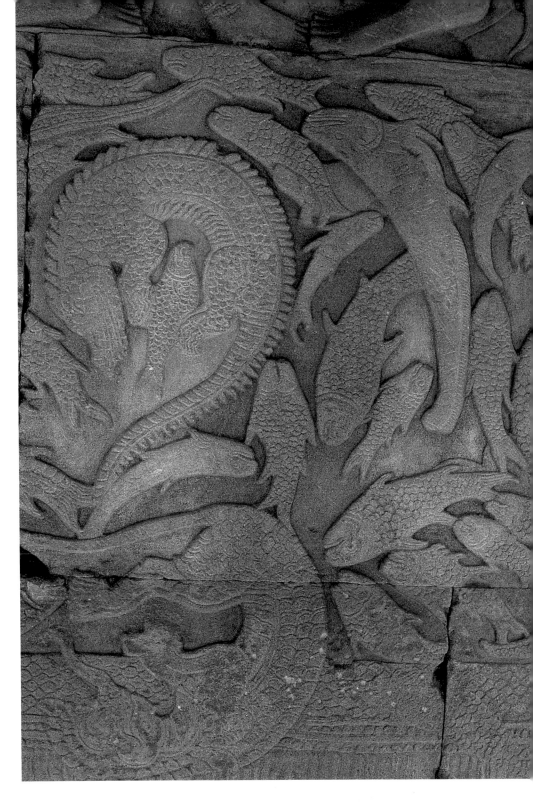

saltwater. He goes further to suggest that while the Angkor Wat 'Churning of the Ocean of Milk' depicts a fish fauna similar to that of the Tonle Sap, the scene actually depicts a river (presumably the Mekong) with fish swimming upstream from left to right. In analysing the Bayon reliefs he has also hypothesised that based on the identification of one fish species – the Bump-headed Carp –, two of the historic naval battles depicted probably took place not on the Tonle Sap, but on the Mekong north of Kratie, to where the species is restricted.

Birds and mammals have not been studied in such detail, but several species can be easily recognised. Excellent representations of Green Peafowl, Sarus Cranes and Greater Adjutant storks can all be found on the Bayon. The wildlife around Angkor depicted on the reliefs hasn't changed in 800 years, what has changed is its abundance. The last record of Green Peafowl from the area was more than 60 years ago, whilst the nearest nesting Greater Adjutants are now approximately 70 kilometres away and Sarus Cranes even further. There are four detailed rhinoceros depictions in Angkor, which on the basis of the single horn and the pattern of skin and plates, can be identified as Javan Rhinoceros. The last confirmed Javan Rhinoceros in Cambodia was shot in 1930[7]. Tyson Roberts found two depictions in the Angkor Wat 'Churning of the Ocean of Milk' of the Large-tooth Sawfish, this is now nearly absent from the Mekong Basin and has not been reported from the Tonle Sap for several decades[8, 9].

What caused species like these to disappear, or become so rare, and when did this happen? Modern accounts of the wildlife of Angkor begin in 1860 with the

French scientist Henri Mouhot. Famed for the 'rediscovery' of Angkor, he was in fact primarily a natural historian. His expedition was supported by, among others, the Zoological Society of London for whom he spent much time collecting specimens, particularly of birds. French ornithologists visited Angkor again during the 1920s, 30s and 40s[10], so there exists an excellent record of birds from that period. This historical information demonstrates that all of the species lost from Angkor have disappeared within the last one hundred years, most within the last fifty. Ornithologist Frédéric Goes has documented thirty-eight species of forest bird previously noted from Angkor that have not been seen since 1960[11].

Hunting has always occurred around Angkor and literary evidence exists for one interesting, but long forgotten, quarry – kingfishers. Kingfisher feathers were highly valued in China, being used both in fashion accessories and to create stunningly beautiful pieces of artwork. Such objects were favoured by high-society and high prices were paid for the feathers. Chou Ta Koun, the 13th century Chinese envoy, reported that Angkor had specialist kingfisher hunters who used caged birds as lures. It has even been suggested that much of the Khmer economy at that time may have been based on trading kingfisher feathers to China[12]. Today four species of kingfisher can be commonly seen as splashes of blue around the forested moats and ponds, but fortunately the trade is long over, and unlike many other birds, they are no longer at risk.

Various bas-reliefs depict hunters with blow-pipes or bow and arrow, and fishermen with cast-nets or spears. The real change has come in the 20th century, as patterns of hunting and trade have been fundamentally altered by access to new technology and new markets. Large birds and mammals are easy targets for a modern hunter armed with a gun, and once killed, an animal can now be in a major market within the day. The advent of nylon monofilament has not only led to gill-nets that have brought the Large-tooth Sawfish to the point of extinction in the Mekong, but also mist-nets that are deployed with frightening success on flying-foxes and birds throughout the country, including within the Angkor Park itself.

At Angkor the affects of hunting are exacerbated by the limited extent of the remaining habitat. It is likely that when the Khmers first settled Angkor, they found a plain of open deciduous dipterocarp forest, with a mosaic of semi-evergreen or evergreen forest in areas of better soil or permanent water. It may have looked much as some areas of Kompong Thom and Preah Vihear do today. Unfortunately the 40-square-kilometre forest-island of present-day Angkor is simply not big enough for the large mammals, such as Tigers, Asian Elephants and Sambar deer that roamed the area in the past. While populations of these animals do remain in forest to the north, they are too far away, and habitation, cultivation and roads mean that linking these areas up is no longer possible. However, effective control of hunting could still bring the return to Angkor of healthy populations of many of the birds and smaller mammals, such as the flying-foxes.

The next group of animals from the walls of Angkor that face extinction are the turtles and tortoises. Found throughout the bas-reliefs, and associated with many of the fish scenes, the turtles are difficult to identify to individual species. They occupy a special position in Cambodian mythology. In the 'Churning of the Ocean of Milk', it was as Kurma, his tortoise incarnation, that Vishnu appeared to prevent Mount Meru from sinking during the violent churning. Turtles are still revered by today's Buddhist society and there is great merit attached to releasing a turtle. Perhaps paradoxically, they are also one of the most threatened groups of animals in Southeast Asia, with a huge legal and illegal trade to supply food and medicinal markets in China. The Cambodian government has recently taken a strong stand against this international trade and has made several major seizures of turtle shipments.

In many ways the international black-market wildlife trade, both of turtles and of higher value species such as Tigers and Asian Elephants, is similar to the illegal trade in looted Angkorian artefacts. With the steady demand from wealthy out of country buyers, both are hugely lucrative for those involved and therefore well worth the risk of being caught. For Cambodia, both are also hugely destructive to the country's cultural and natural heritage. Important artefacts are removed from their setting and lost forever into secretive private collections, whilst animals are hunted and traded, some now to the point of extinction.

The documented looting of temples to supply an international market has been going on since the turn of the 20th century. In 1923 André Malraux set sail from Paris with the express purpose of taking sculptures from Banteay Srei and selling them in America. Fortunately this attempt was foiled when he was arrested in Phnom Penh,

Two representations of hunters in the forest, bas reliefs, Bayon south gallery

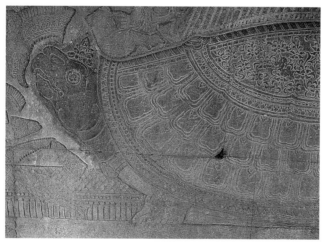

and the pieces were subsequently restored to Banteay Srei. However, things have worsened significantly in recent years, particularly since the early nineties, when the arrival of the UN marked the beginning of Cambodia's road to peace, and 'safe' access to many areas became possible.

Outlying temples have been particularly badly affected and Banteay Chhmar, close to the Thai border, has probably been the most seriously desecrated. There is now new hope in international agreements and several recent high-profile seizures of artefacts, particularly in Thailand. Over the past few years a number of important pieces have been returned, including a major section Banteay Chhmar, and are now in the National Museum in Phnom Penh. One day perhaps when the threat no longer

remains, or the temple is securely protected, they can be restored to where they belong.

For Cambodia's national animal the story is similar, although the end more final. The Kouprey, a long-legged wild forest cow, had always had a range largely confined to Cambodia. It was only discovered by scientists in 1937 and was declared Cambodia's national animal by King Norodom Sihanouk in 1964. Unfortunately it has long been sought after for its impressive horns and the last confirmed sighting was in 1969. It is unlikely that the Kouprey survives anywhere in the country and once gone, it can never be brought back. Probably all that is now left of this magnificent animal are sets of horns, almost all of those in collections outside of Cambodia.

The root cause of both types of loss is similar, as the heritage policemen guarding the temples are paid about the same as rangers protecting national parks. At less than $20 per month, there is a lot of incentive to turn a blind eye, or even be involved in such illegal activity, especially if it is unlikely you will be held to account. The military have long been implicated in much of the country's illegal logging and hunting activities, and witnesses to the 1990s looting at Banteay Chhmar reported the involvement of soldiers with heavy machinery. Once the ill-gotten gains are acquired there is a network of well-established traders and middlemen who will traffic anything out of the country for profit. Cambodia's borders are porous and difficult to police, and it is easy to conceal a stolen Vishnu head, a sack full of turtles or a tiger skin in a truck piled with produce.

All is not yet lost, and there are many Cambodians who understand the true value of their heritage and are fighting to make a difference. What they need is better support, politically and financially. Government staff protecting the country's resources need to be paid a fair salary for their work, such that they need not moonlight with a second job. This would reduce the incentive for corruption. NGOs supporting the government in biodiversity conservation are pioneering the way by providing equipment and salaries to protected area rangers, but if this is to be sustainable it has to be a very long-term commitment. After all, the Cambodian government is unlikely to be in a position to increase civil service salaries to an appropriate level for some time to come.

The relationship between people and the forests of Angkor isn't just one of plunder and profit. Recent anthropological research among communities within the

LEFT:
**One of the few ever pictures of Kouprey in the wild, taken from an 8mm movie shot by Charles Wharton in Preah Vihear in 1952. It shows a group of animals with an adult male to left of the picture with its characteristic pronounced dewlap**
**©WCS**

ABOVE:
**A missing section of wall taken by thieves from Banteay Chhmar temple, part of which has since been returned to National Museum in Phnom Penh**

Angkor Park has shown that many villagers claim customary rights to collect local products going back generations. These include firewood, resin, fruits, wild potatoes, vines, rattans and medicinal herbs from the forest, and fish and crabs from the temple moats[13]. Many of these practises have not changed since Angkorian times. In the wet season small boys using bamboo traps catch fish or crabs in the moat in front of the Bayon bas-reliefs that show their ancestors fishing with cast nets. Not only the environment but the technology, has hardly moved on in 800 years.

All this came to a halt in 2000 when the exploitation of all forest products, including cattle grazing, was banned within Angkor by APSARA, the authority responsible for its management. The number of people living in and around the Angkor Park is continually growing, and as tourism increases and the area prospers more will arrive hoping to improve their livelihoods. The government has recently again taken action by relocating 'squatter' communities outside the park, but this is only a temporarily solution to a complicated problem. Villagers have always been an important part of the long relationship between people and Angkor, and the park may well be better conserved by somehow managing this living history, rather than creating a restricted access museum.

For scholars of Angkor, one of the most controversial aspects of the relationship between the ancient people and their environment has been the management, or not, of water. What is indisputable is that the kings of Angkor constructed a vast water-management system, what is still fiercely argued to this day is why.

A young girl with crab she caught from the moat of the Bayon temple

ABOVE:
**Local women collecting
firewood from within the
Angkor park**

RIGHT:
**Collecting grass for animal
fodder in front of the Elephant
Terrace**

**Planting rice in front of Pre Rup temple**

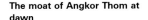

To the north of the road east out of Angkor Wat, where it crosses the Siem Reap River, is a water wheel. It has not been placed there as a tourist attraction, but to lift water from the river to irrigate a tree nursery managed by the provincial forestry office. Although the tree nursery is a recent addition, the use of water wheels like this has changed little since the great Angkorian kings were processing by on their elephant many hundreds of years ago.

The academic discussion, however, is about water management at a much larger order of magnitude. Over a period of more than three hundred years between the ninth and twelfth centuries, the kings of Angkor constructed a series of vast reservoirs, or *barays*. Bernard-Philippe Groslier, French scholar and conservator of Angkor until the early 1970s, first advanced the theory of Angkor as a 'hydraulic city'. The *barays*, he claimed, were a key part of a massive centralised water storage and distribution scheme. They irrigated rice fields over a wide area, supporting an enormous population and enabling the development of a vast empire. In the early 1980s, Dutch water engineer W.J. van Liere, questioned the feasibility of this on technical grounds, and debate has continued ever since.

Now modern techniques of satellite imagery, computer modelling and AIRSAR aerial radar survey, the latter carried out at great expense by NASA, are shedding new light on this old conundrum. An examination of the hydrology of the Kulen range suggests that during the 10th or 11th centuries a number of off-take canals were dug diverting water directly south. One of these, possibly the first, was the current Siem Reap River[14], perhaps more accurately now to be called the Siem Reap Canal? It has been proposed that this may have been built to supply the East Baray with water, while another channel further west, the Great North Channel, less visible in today's landscape, was built to feed the West Baray.

With the new evidence revealing, and mapping, such extensive canal systems the issue will continue to rage on. But while the debate is polarised around irrigation, other perhaps equally important functions of these canals and *barays* should not be overlooked.

The *barays* weren't reservoirs dug into the ground, but were created by building above ground embankments to hold back and store wet season water flowing across the landscape to the Tonle Sap. They were vast shallow 'Oceans' each oriented east-west and including its own

Cast-net fishermen, crocodiles and turtles, bas relief, Bayon temple south gallery

ABOVE:
**Extensive lotus cultivation fields from the air, Kompong Chhnang**

RIGHT:
**A lotus flower, Chong Kneas, Siem Reap**

island temple – 'Mount Meru'. With the religious importance of water to the ancient Khmers, the cosmological role of the *barays* was probably as important as any other. If the kings of Angkor were able to engineer such great monuments to the gods in stone, why not also in water?

Perhaps the canals were primarily constructed for transportation? Much of the rock, both sandstone and laterite, used to build the temples came from the Kulen range or its foothills. How were these heavy stones moved to Angkor? One of the Bayon bas-reliefs shows rock being quarried and hauled away by elephants[15], but did elephants then drag them more than 30 kilometres to Angkor? It has been suggested instead that elephants were used to transport these blocks to the Siem Reap River where they were placed onto bamboo rafts and floated to the building sites downstream[16]. Perhaps the construction of the Siem Reap Canal was necessary to deliver the stone to the relevant temple site, or without the canal, maybe the river was not navigable, throughout the year, for the size of raft needed? Again in comparison to their major engineering feats, the construction of a canal for such a purpose would have been easy for the Khmers of Angkor.

Another possible role for the *barays* has been suggested by botanist Andrew McDonald, who has completed a detailed ecological and cultural study of the lotus. He has proposed that the ceremonial demand for lotus flowers throughout the Angkor period was such that it would have required cultivation of the plants on an industrial scale. Today lotus is farmed in wetlands across Cambodia and perhaps some of the *barays* could have been ancient lotus farms?

Cast-net fishermen, Ang
Trapeang Thmor, Banteay
Meanchey

**Khmer dancer depicting a mythical 'mermaid' in a traditional dance, Preah Khan temple**

But to return to the 'photographs of past', the most obvious thing that the bas-reliefs show us is the importance of fish to the Angkorian civilisation. There are thousands of individual accurately-drawn fish decorating temples from every period. There are also multiple depictions of people catching fish, trading fish and cooking fish, far more than there are of any other environment related economic activity, including anything linked to rice. We can safely draw the conclusion that fish was as important a protein source to Cambodians then as it is now. Whether specifically designed for the purpose or not, the *barays* would have undoubtedly functioned as large aquaculture reservoirs, and perhaps the ancient Khmers were really fish farmers rather than rice farmers?

In reality, as pointed out by hydrologist Matti Kummu, the water management systems of Angkor were almost certainly multi-functional, being used not only for everything mentioned above, but also washing, sanitation, defence and no doubt many other purposes.

Water, whether for religious ceremonies, fisheries, rice agriculture or all of the above and more, undoubtedly formed the central basis of the Angkorian civilization and economy. Groslier believed it to be so important that he blamed the demise of the water management system for the decline of Angkor. Again, there are many theories as to the demise of Angkor, but today, archaeologists Roland Fletcher and Christophe Pottier suggest that Groslier may well have been right. They believe that the new imagery provides evidence of siltation and erosion that would have gradually destroyed the water management system and led to the decline of the economy and therefore the empire[17].

Management of water continues to be a growing problem for people and Angkor today. Even despite the affects of SARS on regional tourism, total foreign visitors to Angkor in 2003 exceeded 320,000, and with direct flights to Siem Reap existing or planned from nine countries, annual tourist figures at Angkor are projected very soon to rise to over one million. Managing both the number of tourists and the number of people needed to provide them with the facilities and services they require, is the next challenge. It is estimated that each tourist requires approximately 500 litres of clean water per day. Not only is the Siem Reap River insufficient to supply what is required[18], but it is reported that the water from the pumping station is polluted by the city sewers. To ensure a supply of clean water to Siem Reap the government has, with donor funding from Japan, embarked on a $10 million water supply project. In addition work has also begun on a $3.5 million sewage treatment system, financed by the Asian Development Bank.

These are essential, as neither the temple complex itself, nor the surrounding city, can handle the numbers of people that are currently arriving, never mind those that are forecast. Without urgent action on a whole range of levels, the story of the relationship between people and Angkor may be heading for another catastrophe. This time the role of the inability of the water management system to cope with the demands of a growing population is already documented, and would not be debatable.

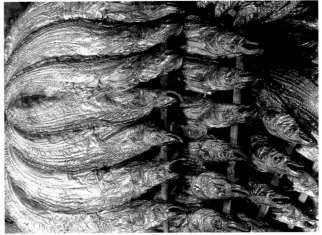

# FOOD FOR THE VULTURES

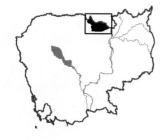

Chou Ta Koun reported that in the 13th century, when a Cambodian died the corpse was carried to a remote place outside of the city and abandoned for vultures and other beasts to devour. This is similar to the practise of sky burial still carried out by present-day Tibetans and the Parsees of India. However, the decline of vultures means that if the same custom was to be continued today, a corpse would have to be taken 200 kilometres from Angkor before there would be sufficient birds for its disposal.

Vultures have declined significantly in Cambodia during the course of this century. At one time distributed widely across the north of the country, the stronghold for vultures has always been the open deciduous dipterocarp forests of the northern plains, both east and west of the Mekong. This is a landscape where four species of wild cattle (including the probably extinct Kouprey) once roamed. It is a land that was described as late as 1957 by biologist Charles Wharton as "one of the great gamelands

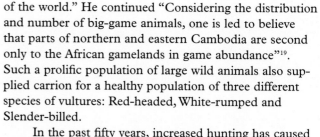

of the world." He continued "Considering the distribution and number of big-game animals, one is led to believe that parts of northern and eastern Cambodia are second only to the African gamelands in game abundance"[19]. Such a prolific population of large wild animals also supplied carrion for a healthy population of three different species of vultures: Red-headed, White-rumped and Slender-billed.

In the past fifty years, increased hunting has caused wild cattle populations to crash and, starved of their major food supply, so have vultures. In an unrelated event, vultures in the Indian sub-continent have undergone even steeper declines, decreasing by over 90% in some areas, due to a drug, diclofenac, that is used in domestic cattle but is inadvertently toxic to vultures. Indications are that Cambodia is thankfully free of this drug for veterinary use, making the populations remaining in Cambodia of even greater global importance. This is particularly so in the case of Slender-billed Vulture, with the Cambodian population probably being the most significant left in the world.

In response to this conservationists in Cambodia have adopted an innovative approach not previously tried in Southeast Asia. In conjunction with local communities they have set up a program to provide supplementary food for the vultures. Working with local villagers, sick cattle and buffalo are purchased, slaughtered and left for the vultures. The program is already proving successful and a monitoring program has recorded significant numbers of vultures visiting a number of such 'restaurants'. In addition several birds have now been marked with coloured tags and satellite transmitters as part of a research program to better understand their movements and distribution. This is just a small part of a major project initiated by the government and WCS with support from the Global Environment Facility of UNDP. It aims, over the next ten years, to initiate a series of long-term conservation interventions that will conserve key areas for wildlife and help endangered species such as the vultures and wild cattle recover, across the landscape of the northern plains.

**A smouldering log and cycad in deciduous dipterocarp forest, Preah Vihear**

LEFT:
**Vultures (predominantly White-rumped Vultures) at a feeding restaurant, Preah Vihear**

BELOW LEFT
**Mixed group of vultures (upper bird Slender-billed Vulture) at a feeding restaurant, Preah Vihear**

BELOW RIGHT:
**Monks travelling by ox-cart through the deciduous dipterocarp forest, Preah Vihear**

# PHNOM KRAOM AND THE FLOODPLAIN

RIGHT:
**Phnom Kraom from the Tonle Sap in the wet season**

OPPOSITE PAGE:
**Sunrise from Phnom Kraom in the wet season**

For ancient Khmers approaching Phnom Kraom across the Tonle Sap in the wet season, it must have looked like the real Mount Meru rising above one of the greatest oceans of all. At its summit sits a small three-tiered temple, built in the late 9th century under the reign of King Yasovarman I. From this 140m vantage point, between August and December, the water of the Tonle Sap stretches for kilometres and kilometres around, giving a view of what is without question the largest lake in Southeast Asia.

While in the dry season the Tonle Sap lake 'only' stretches for approximately 150 kilometres in length and averages around 20 kilometres in width, new radar satellite imagery has revealed the true extent of the lake's flood. At the peak of the wet season the Tonle Sap can expand to 250 kilometres long and in places more than 100 kilometres wide. The lake is shallow, measuring only 1-2 metres at its deepest in the dry season, rising to more than 10 metres in the wet season. As a result as it floods the total inundated area increases four-fold, from 2,500 square kilometres to over 13,000 square kilometres.

Several times over the past million years what is now the Tonle Sap would have been at the bottom of a vast shallow marine sea, and the formation of the lake itself is, in geological time, very young. The Tonle Sap lies on a northwest-southeast geological fault line and was created by the subsidence of the 'Cambodian platform' around 5,700 years ago. There has been little or no geological activity in the area since then and it is likely that the Tonle Sap of today is very similar in size and shape to the lake the Angkorians would have known.

Angkor is on one of the narrowest and steepest parts of the Tonle Sap floodplain. Positioned just above the maximum wet season water level, it is perfectly located to take advantage of the lake throughout the year, yet not be at risk from flooding. Today from the summit of Phnom Kraom almost every meter of land, from the shores of the Tonle Sap to Angkor and beyond, is devoted to rice agriculture.

Cultivated rice has its origins in Asia and archaeologist Charles Higham believes the first rice farmers arrived in South-east Asia about 4,300 years ago[20]. Cambodians have been growing rice in the Tonle Sap floodplain for well over 2,000 years. Over centuries of floods and droughts, a broad range of plants adapted to local conditions has evolved, making the Mekong Basin one of the world's centres of rice diversity with over 2,000 rice varieties identified as unique to Cambodia alone[21].

The Khmer Rouge Government of Pol Pot, however, had a devastating affect on agricultural production from which the country is still recovering. The regime aimed to increase rice production and treble yields. Redundant forest lands were to be cleared, new one hectare standard-sized rice fields created and high yield crop varieties introduced with the help of Chinese advisors. It was a total disaster – national rice surpluses never materialised and as a result millions perished of starvation. Much local knowledge and traditional seed stock was lost.

Cambodia has four basic rice ecosystems: deepwater, dry season irrigated and recession, rainfed lowland and rainfed upland. These occur in continuous belts around the Tonle Sap, the deepwater rice being closest to the lake, then a band of irrigated recession rice, followed, above the level of the maximum flood, by rainfed rice and finally, well away from the lake, upland rice. The predominant form of rice agriculture throughout the country is rainfed lowland rice deriving its water from rain or local run off. Official figures show that in every year since 1994 this crop has made up around 90% of the national harvest[22].

LEFT:
**Farmers working field of recently planted rice, Kompong Cham**

BELOW:
**Transplanting rice seedlings, Kompong Cham**

BELOW RIGHT:
**Dry season harvested rice fields from the air, Prey Veng**

The annual Cambodian cycle begins with New Year in mid-April. This is the hottest, driest time of year, all agricultural activities have finished and there is plenty of time to party. Although the official holiday only lasts three days, across the country traditional festivities last up to a month as people celebrate and give thanks for the year gone before. The land is parched and hard, the rice stubble remaining after a dry season of grazing has been burned, and everybody is waiting for the first rains of the coming year. In May, after celebrations are over, the first monsoon rains begin. After the water soaks far enough into the soil to enable ploughing by cattle or water buffalo, land preparation commences and rice seedbeds are established. When the seed is in the ground rural Cambodia's annual cycle of life starts again.

Transplanting is the predominant method of establishing the crop. Seedbeds are first created in small areas where the early water can be reliably controlled. The age at which seedlings are transplanted is flexible, anywhere from 20 to 90 days, dependent upon the rice variety and environmental conditions. This flexibility is essential as rain and therefore the water supply is never totally predictable. Fields are ploughed twice in preparation for

**Transporting rice seedling to fields by ox-cart, Kompong Cham**

**Bringing in the harvested rice, Ang Trapeang Thmor, Banteay Meanchey**

transplanting, the first time to destroy weeds and the second to ready the field for the seedlings. Depending upon the rains, transplanting will usually be carried out in July or August.

Rice is usually 'photoperiod sensitive', as the timing of flowering is governed by day length rather than other variables. When over 1,500, predominantly traditional, Cambodian rice varieties were analysed in 1994, it was found that well over 90% were strongly photoperiod sensitive[23]. This adaptation allows the crop to be planted according to the availability of the rain, yet still flower in September or October when there is least likely to be drought. The harvest follows about five weeks after flowering, from mid-November through January, and is still largely carried out by hand.

Deepwater rice is also strongly photoperiod sensitive, and is thought to be close to the ancestral stock from which all common rainfed lowland rice varieties evolved. It is highly diverse, with thousands of different varieties for specific flood conditions and water regimes. Agronomist David Catling estimates that there are 6,500 genotypes of deepwater rice in Asia of which 500 originated in Cambodia[24]. Deepwater rice is defined as growing in an area usually flooded deeper than 50cm for one month or longer during the growing season. In Cambodia it can be divided into two types: floating and traditional tall. Floating rice grows in areas where the water depth is greater than 100cm for one month or longer. Plants survive by growing the stem as the water rises, sometimes up to 5-6m. The stems are hollow with large air spaces and float on the water surface. Traditional tall rice grows in shallower areas and survives by its tall stature and long leaves. These are the only crops which tolerate such deep flooding conditions.

Land preparation for floating rice begins in February and March, burning stubble and scrub in preparation for ploughing. Ploughing is often difficult, due to regenerating scrub and dry soil, and tractors are usually used, particularly in areas around the Tonle Sap. Floating rice is never transplanted and seed is broadcast manually between May and mid-June, depending upon the rainfall. Fertilizers are never used and pesticides only rarely[25]. Harvesting is carried out during January and February, and is done with hand-sickles. Due to the photoperiod sensitivity, the start of the harvest depends upon the rice variety used rather than the timing of the flood recession.

LEFT:
Old lady winnowing rice,
Kompong Thom

BOTTOM:
Rice seller, Tbeng Meanchay,
Preah Vihear

BELOW:
Bunches of cut rice seedlings
ready for transplanting

**Travelling through wet season deepwater rice fields, Kompong Thom**

Deepwater rice has been grown by Cambodians for centuries, being first mentioned in connection with Angkor in the 13th century. In the 1930s the area planted was estimated at 540,000ha. It remained high during the 1960s, but recent figures indicate that only 70,000ha remains, less than 1% of the total crop. It is grown closest to the lake, in areas that could otherwise not be cultivated, and today the majority is in Kompong Thom. Deepwater rice varieties have lower yields than other ones, but require very low inputs. Most deepwater rice farmers have limited resources, but in an environment of extreme flood and drought, the crop provides for their basic subsistence needs.

Nevertheless there are some risks in deepwater rice farming. The growth rate is determined by the speed at which the water rises and a floating rice plant can elongate at up to 20-30cm per day. However, a rapid, continuous water rise at the wrong time, particularly during flowering, can submerge the plant and kill it, resulting in the failure of the total crop[26]. Rats are also a significant problem, particularly for today's deepwater rice farmers. They can devastate the crop both during and after flooding. This problem has apparently been exacerbated by the persecution of natural predators such as snakes and birds[27].

In the deepwater rice areas of Kompong Thom, an innovative approach has linked pest control to wildlife conservation and traditional Cambodian culture. Hong Chamnan, a government official from the Forestry Administration with support from WCS, manages a project to conserve the threatened birds of one of Cambodia's oldest, ecosystems. To the south of Kompong Thom town, perhaps more than any other part of the Tonle Sap floodplain, the rice agriculture system has changed little over hundreds, or even thousands, of years.

The area consists of more than 1,600 square kilometres of seasonally flooded grasslands and scrub, interspersed with deepwater rice. It is a landscape shaped by grazing, burning and, where deepwater rice is farmed, ploughing. Uninhabitable for six months of the year, as it is inundated by up to several metres of water, people start to return to the area in January. In addition to the local deepwater rice farmers, temporary migrants from upland areas move many kilometres by ox-cart in search of good grazing for their cattle. By February and March more than three hundred ox-carts and five thousand cattle have been counted in the area. Throughout the dry season burning is also a common occurrence with fires set to

ABOVE:
**Selling rice field water birds (including Watercock bottom right), Psa Kraom, Siem Reap**

RIGHT:
**Cooked water birds, Tvang, Battambang**

clear land before ploughing or to ease access into new areas. It is difficult to separate out the relative roles of these three processes, ploughing, grazing and burning, in shaping the habitat we see today. It is likely they have all been practised for centuries and perhaps at one time an ecosystem such as this stretched to the delta?

This vast swathe of remnant habitat supports a whole suite of threatened bird species, now largely absent from the rest of the region. Foremost among these is the Bengal Florican, a large long-legged grassland bird of the bustard family. Classified as globally Critically Endangered by IUCN, it is found in only two areas: a restricted part of India and Nepal and in the Mekong floodplain. Here, north of the Tonle Sap is the largest population in the world, perhaps consisting of more than several hundred birds. During the dry season males can be seen displaying and defending territories where the deepwater rice and natural grass breaks up the scrub.

They are not the only endangered birds here, as there are a number of other important resident and migrant species. As the water rises and the floricans move to higher ground, the area becomes an important feeding area for storks and ibises that breed elsewhere around the Tonle Sap. They arrive in large numbers to feed on the invertebrates, frogs and rodents flushed out by the returning flood. During the winter months the area is significant for at least two species of globally-endangered raptor from China and Russia: Great Spotted and Imperial Eagles. Large numbers of birds of prey use the area in the dry season, feasting primarily on rodents. Sarus Cranes also arrive at this time, moving away from their breeding grounds to the north to search for invertebrates and tubers in the wetter areas closer to the lake.

Current populations of these birds are but a fraction of their former levels. What little information there is from the area, indicates that historically all these birds were once more common. The key factor driving their decline has been hunting, as they are large, slow and easy to catch, particularly at night, even using hand nets.

When he started discussing these issues with local communities, Hong Chamnan soon found that his greatest allies were village elders. They remembered a time when there were many more birds and far fewer pests, both invertebrates and rodents. Chamnan designed an environmental education program around this scenario linking levels of bird hunting to those of crop pests, and he has

developed uniquely Cambodian ways of doing this. One of the most popular is a traditional travelling shadow puppet theatre which visits villages with a historical tale based around farming, hunting and Khmer mythology. This has attracted crowds of up to 2,000 people. It's a shining example of what is possible. Without any law enforcement activities in the area bird hunting has successfully been reduced to negligible levels.

In addition, on-going research in Kompong Thom indicates that the small rice farming areas are actually preferred by the floricans. Chamnan and his team are now aiming to work with local farmers to develop ways to maintain their traditional deepwater rice livelihoods, with the added benefit of supporting florican conservation. However, many of the areas are now being threatened by large-scale conversion to recession rice.

Before a project such as this can discuss hunting issues with rural communities, it is essential to first understand local livelihoods and protein sources. In Kompong Thom, this was not too difficult, as like rice farmers throughout Cambodia, everybody relied on fish. The total fish production for Cambodia is more than 400,000 tons per year, and fish is estimated to provide over 80% of protein intake across the country. Deepwater rice areas have long been known to represent a diverse fishery, and although its value has never been estimated.

Recent work has revealed the true importance of rice field fisheries. It is difficult to calculate the real economic value of the rice field catch as most of it is for household consumption and never reaches market. However research from Svay Rieng estimated a productivity of up to 125 kg

Catching snakes in a rice field,
Kompong Thom

of fish per ha of rice field. Figures from other areas have ranged from 25-61 kg per ha, and if this were multiplied by the total area of Cambodia's lowland rice fields it could reach a minimum annual production of more than 100,000 tons, or 25% of the total annual fish catch[28, 29]. In addition, people harvest countless other frogs, crabs, snakes and insects from the rice field, whose significance has never been assessed. The importance of this fishery to national food security and the rural economy can not be denied. In some areas the value of wild-caught fish from rice fields exceeds the value of rice. Maybe Cambodians could more accurately be described as fishermen who also farm, rather than farmers who also fish?

However, this rice-fish co-productivity may be threatened by new agricultural developments. Dry season rice has long made up only a small proportion of Cambodia's total crop, usually comprising less than 10% of the total area under rice, but it is now increasing. There are two different forms. The first, and most common, is partially-irrigated flood recession rice. Water from the receding flood is held back for distribution to the fields. Sowing is staggered from as early as the end of October to as late as March, depending on the depth of flood and the timing of the recession.

The second form is irrigated, dry season rice, a second crop produced after the first wet season rainfed rice. As Cambodians look for greater productivity through intensification and the option of a second crop, this is of increasing importance, particularly with introduction of new high-yielding rice varieties (HYV). To maximise yields these modern varieties grow best under a controlled regime of water supply and chemical application. However, increasing pesticide use results in decreasing fish populations[30] and the most intensively farmed areas support little life other than the rice itself.

Before 1990 agricultural chemicals were not readily available in Cambodia, but as the country opened up to the outside world this changed. Between 1989 and 1999 pesticide imports more than doubled[31]. No policy existed and dangerous chemicals banned in other countries were imported. However, all was not quite what it seemed. In 1995 of 22 products tested from markets around Phnom Penh, only five were of the claimed strength or above. Half were below 55% of the claimed strength and eight possessed either none or little of the active ingredient[32]. A 1999 study of toxic residues in fish found DDT levels were low, with the highest values recorded from Kompong Chhnang. The researchers concluded that residue levels were lower than in other parts of Asia, and that Cambodia was one of the cleanest countries in the region[33].

But it may be difficult for Cambodia to keep its enviable status, as a recent report by the UK NGO, the Environmental Justice Foundation, found the use of hazardous pesticides to be increasing across the country. In 2000 it was estimated that 1.3 million litres of pesticides were used in the Tonle Sap catchment, involving 76 different compounds in 241 different products. 33% of these pesticides are classified by the World Health Organisation as Class One: highly or extremely hazardous to human health. In most provinces, the most commonly used pesticides were all WHO Class One chemicals. Of the 241 products, 42 were banned in Vietnam, one of the main sources for pesticides in Cambodia[34]. These pesticides will not only negatively affect the biodiversity of the agro-ecosystem, they are poisoning farmers and their families, creating pest resurgence and consequently a greater dependency on increasing external inputs.

An alternative way forward is being provided by integrated pest management (IPM), the objective of which is to encourage natural pest control methods. It involves minimising the use of pesticides by adopting a range of approaches and interventions to pest management, some chemical, but others biological, cultural or temporal. IPM is now being widely promoted in Cambodia by the UN Food and Agriculture Organisation (FAO) and a range of other donors. By 2002 over 30,000 Cambodian farmers had attended 'farmer field schools' to learn about IPM and were carrying the knowledge back to others in their communities[35]. Linked to this is the promotion of rice-fish culture systems, as fish are both beneficial in pest control and increased fish production raises farmers' livelihoods. Fisheries biologist Rick Gregory suggested that IPM

**Hong Chamnan and WCS field research team at work, Kompong Thom**

programmes would benefit from replacing the negative message "do not spray" with a positive one "stock fish"[36].

Such initiatives should be encouraged, because if present intensification continues, many traditional forms of agriculture will be lost. The location of Angkor made it possible to maintain a diversity of rice ecosystems. Floating rice was harvested from the lake; rain-fed cultivation could be carried out across much of the lowland plain; small-scale upland cultivation would have been possible to the north in the foothills of Kulen; and some form of irrigation, however limited or extensive, could have held water back for an additional, dry season crop. Maintaining this diversity over centuries has helped Cambodians survive through a strategy of minimising risk rather than maximising profit.

The danger now is that the ancient diverse and productive rice-growing areas around the Tonle Sap will go the same way as Thailand's Chao Phraya River basin. Much of Thailand's central plain is now a sterile rice monoculture, scarcely supporting any natural life. Areas which used to grow a single crop of traditional deepwater rice have been converted into fields of HYV rice producing two or even three crops a year. Ornithologist Philip Round recently described these areas as follows: "Emerald green rice paddies look pleasing to the eye . . . But their superficial beauty cannot hide the fraying of Thailand's rich rural tapestry, encompassing landscape, tradition, culture and biodiversity, into a threadbare, agro-industrial ragpile"[37]. It would be a tragedy if the lowland agricultural floodplain diversity that has been a treasure of Cambodia since before Angkor were to go the same way.

# THE CRANES OF BANTEAY MEANCHEY

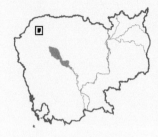

Banteay Meanchey, Cambodia's north-western province has a special affinity with the most charismatic of Cambodian grassland birds; the Sarus Crane. It is here, at Banteay Chhmar, a remote temple close to the Thai border that the story of cranes and Cambodia begins.

On a low pediment over the main entrance from the east, is an image incorporating two cranes, their necks pierced by an arrow. Sadly, two of the faces have now been stolen, but Angkorian scholar Vittorio Roveda has been able to interpret the relief as illustrating the very beginning of the *Ramayana*. The relief shows Valmiki, the

**Lintel depicting the killing of two cranes and the beginning of the Ramayana, Banteay Chhmar temple**

author of this epic poem, witnessing a tribal hunter killing a pair of cranes. On his left Brahma is handing him a pen and commanding him to convert this emotional experience into poetry for the edification of man[38]. It was then he created the Ramayana, scenes from which are depicted around the galleries of Angkor Wat and many other Khmer temples.

Not far east of Banteay Chhmar, along the ancient Angkorian road leading back to Siem Reap, lies one of the most disastrous pieces of engineering in Cambodian history – the vast dam of Ang Trapeang Thmor. This nineteen kilometre-long dyke was one the most ambitious irrigation schemes attempted by the Khmer Rouge. As part of his agrarian revolution Pol Pot tried to mimic what he saw as the great centrally-operated water systems of the Angkorian kings. At Ang Trapeang Thmor the intention was to form a large reservoir by creating a dyke along the ancient Angkorian road. As with everything associated with this period, it was a human catastrophe, thousands of Cambodians died and the irrigation system was never completed. Today it stands as a monument to the country's tragic past.

However, the reservoir that was created formed a large seasonally flooded grassland perfect for waterbirds. In 1998 the late Sam Veasna, Siem Reap provincial wildlife officer, following up on reports from local people, visited the area for the first time and counted a flock of 198 Sarus Cranes. In response to this discovery in February 2000 the then king, Samdech Norodom Sihanouk, designated the area a 'Crane Conservation Area' by Royal Decree.

Since its declaration, the reserve has been managed by the Forestry Administration with assistance from the International Crane Foundation and WCS. With protection, the cranes, which spend the dry season here, have also increased and currently number over three hundred birds. This is now the largest concentration of Sarus Cranes in Cambodia, and possibly the world. Now not only cranes but thousands of other threatened waterbirds also use the reservoir and from December to February these include huge numbers of ducks: Lesser Whistling Duck, Gargeney and several hundred Comb Duck, the largest population in the region.

TOP:
**Sarus Cranes in flight,
Ang Trapeang Thmor**

ABOVE:
**Hong Chamnan at the Ang
Trapeang Thmor Crane
Conservation Area**

TOP:
**A large flock of Lesser
Whistling Ducks, Ang Trapeang
Thmor**

ABOVE:
**Pair of breeding Sarus Cranes,
Preah Vihear**

# CHONG KNEAS AND PREK TOAL: LIVING ON THE LAKE

RIGHT:
**Houseboat in dry season 'dry dock', Chong Kneas, Siem Reap**

BELOW:
**Moving house, Chong Kneas, Siem Reap**

At the height of the wet season the village of Chong Kneas encircles Phnom Kraom. During the dry season you have to climb to the top of Phnom Kraom even to see it, as it floats, seven kilometres away, on the now distant waters of the Tonle Sap. As the lake advances and retreats, so do the people living on and around it. The 1998 national population census showed 3.5 million people living in the watershed of the Tonle Sap. Over one million of them inhabit the floodplain itself, and like those for centuries before them, these people have developed many strategies for surviving in this hostile environment.

One of the most common adaptations to life on the lake is the floating village. Wooden houses are built upon great mats of bamboo, metal drums or boat hulls, such that the front veranda floats a metre or so above the water. As the lake rises and falls so do the houses. Villages move, not only metres up and down during the year, but also several kilometres back and forth as the Tonle Sap contracts and expands.

Otherwise life in a floating village is much the same as in any Cambodian community. In larger villages the high street is lined with shops, restaurants, hair dressers, fuel stations, karaoke bars and even pagodas – all floating. The only difference is that the street is made of water and people travel by canoe or motor boat rather than bicycle or motorcycle.

A 1997 survey of eight floating villages in the Prek Toal area – across the lake from Chong Kneas at the mouth of Battambang's Sangke River – found that the major source of income for over 90% of people inteviewed was family-scale fishing. Commercial collection of firewood

A floating village from the air, with houseboats, fish cages and floating houses, Kbal Taol, Pursat

was second, followed by animal raising, involving fish, pigs, chickens, ducks and crocodiles[39]. These results are probably typical of the more than 80,000 people living in about 170 similar villages on and around the Tonle Sap[40].

The floating villages are also some of the most ethnically diverse in Cambodia; in addition to Khmer, they contain significant Cham Muslim, Vietnamese and Chinese communities. Traditionally, many floating villages have been inhabited by Vietnamese and about 12,000 are thought to live on the lake, but, as many have no official status, their true numbers are difficult to determine. This diversity among communities is key to their economies, with Cham and Vietnamese invariably seen as the most skillful fishermen[41].

Foreign travellers have been visiting the Tonle Sap for centuries. The shore of the lake that now hosts the floating village of Chong Kneas would have once witnessed maritime trade linking Angkor to the sea. Goods were traded as far afield as China and ports would have bustled with travellers from all over the world. This ancient link to the world died with the demise of the

Travelling down the high street,
Prek Toal, Battambang

FAR LEFT:
**Stilt houses and fish traps in the dry season, Kompong Phluk, Siem Reap**

LEFT:
**Young Brahminy Kites kept as pets, Prek Toal, Battambang**

BELOW:
**Vietnamese noodle seller and
shop, Prek Toal, Battambang**

RIGHT:
**Hanging bedding to dry,
Prek Toal, Battambang**

ABOVE:
**Nuns from the pagoda,
Prek Toal, Battambang**

RIGHT:
**Returning to the village with
firewood cut from the swamp
forest, Prek Toal, Battambang**

FAR RIGHT:
**Vietnamese dentist and captive
Long-tailed Macaque, Prek Toal**

Angkorian civilisation, but Chong Kneas today still functions locally as a port.

Both people and commodities have long been transported between Siem Reap and Phnom Penh by large wooden cargo ships and ferries plying the route across the Tonle Sap. However, with the recent development of Cambodia's road network, lake travel is now decreasing, since a trip that used to take more than two days by boat has now been reduced to less than half a day by bus.

Today the port of Chong Kneas has two major functions. The first is as the most important landing area for fish in the northern part of the Tonle Sap. From small floating communities all over the lake, fish are traded through networks of middlemen ending up at Chong Kneas. From there the catch enters a system of merchants and traders, with most of the high-value fish going directly to Thailand and perhaps eventually ending up in other parts of Asia or even North America. Current data shows that Cambodia exports over 50,000 tons of fish per year, but this is widely acknowledged to be an underestimate[42].

The second role of Chong Kneas is as a passenger terminal, primarily for increasing numbers of foreign tourists making the journey from Phnom Penh to Siem Reap. With the growth of this sector, and the development of more luxurious ferries and cruise vessels, once again the lure of Angkor is creating a port that is a crossroads for international travellers.

Although placed directly over Cambodia's richest natural resource, the floating villages are some of the country's poorest communities. A recent study found that floating villages were generally worse off than their upland

BELOW LEFT:
**Floating pigs and a Long-tailed Macaque, local belief is that pigs are healthier if they are kept with a monkey, Prek Toal, Battambang**

BELOW:
**Throwing fish out to dry, Prek Toal, Battambang**

ABOVE:
**Khmer New Year at a pagoda, Kompong Luong, Pursat**

counterparts. Villagers were less educated, with fewer livelihood options, no agricultural land and a strong dependence on common property resources such as fisheries and swamp forests[43].

Local pollution from organic and faecal waste is a problem, particularly in the larger floating villages. The waters around Chong Kneas, Kompong Luong and Chhnouk Tru are all similarly affected by human effluent, fish-processing waste and garbage. Ironically, while living on the largest lake in the region less than 15% of people in such communities have access to safe drinking water and diarrhoea consequently is one of the leading causes of infant mortality.

Access to effective and affordable services of education and healthcare is a problem throughout Cambodia, and a particular issue on the lake. If students in the villages around Prek Toal wish to study above Fifth Grade they must leave the floating village and go to live in the provincial capital, Battambang[44]. Government health clinics, if available, are rarely staffed by qualified personnel and the astronomical fees charged to sick villagers by unqualified medical practitioners and untrained 'pharmacists' are one of the major causes of family debt.

In recent years crocodile raising has emerged as an important activity in the floating villages. For many however their primary function is not as a commercial venture, but as a savings account. Far away from banks, a crocodile represents the safest investment available to a fisherman with extra cash after a productive season.

Siamese Crocodiles have long been hunted on the Tonle Sap, but the development of crocodile farming for

skins began only after 1945 when the French colonial authorities banned commercial hunting. From the early 1980s to mid-1990s demand from farms in Thailand meant that live crocodiles commanded high prices with hatchlings fetching $300 and an adult female as much as $7,000. After the Asian economic crisis of the late 1990s, and with it a drop in the demand for crocodile leather shoes, the Thai market crashed and prices plummeted. By 2000 hatchlings brought only $25-30 and an adult female $700[45].

Now prices are increasing again, fuelled by a demand from the booming economy of China. Currently there are well over 800 crocodile farms in Cambodia holding more than 4,000 breeding adult females. Official statistics show that registered exports in 2002 exceeded 40,000 animals, primarily to Vietnam and China (and it is likely that most of the animals traded to Vietnam were subsequently re-exported to China). In addition illegal non-registered exports during this period are believed to be significant[46, 47].

Most of the exports are from a few large commercial farms such as the government-run farm in central Siem Reap, that holds thousands of animals. The majority of farms though are small individually-run operations holding only a few animals. The first crocodile farm in Prek Toal was started in 1979 by a local fisherman using wild crocodiles caught from the nearby swamp forest. There are now more than 100 families in the Prek Toal area keeping crocodiles and potentially over 1,000 adult females[48].

As with everything else in Prek Toal, crocodile farms must float, and floating crocodile pens are believed to be

Elder from the pagoda blessing
a family with the water of the
lake, Prek Toal

unique to the villages of the lake. The animals are kept in wooden cages, adjacent to the owner's house. When the water drops, temporary breeding enclosures are constructed on land and the animals are taken ashore to nest. After the females have laid eggs and the water rises again, they are returned to the floating pens. The eggs are collected, incubated and the young hatchlings placed in separate floating pens.

Most families keeping crocodiles in the villages have little knowledge of farming techniques. Animals are kept in poor conditions at densities that are far too high and this is reflected in their productivity. A recent study showed that only 40% of females nested annually and the hatching rate from eggs laid was only a 50%[49].

Hunting crocodiles to stock farms remains the greatest current threat to Siamese Crocodiles throughout the country. Recent surveys in the Core Areas of the Tonle Sap have failed to reveal any significant signs of wild crocodiles[50], and it may well be that infrequent local reports actually relate to animals escaped from village farms. Unless urgent action is taken crocodiles will soon be lost as a wild animal, not just from the Tonle Sap, but across Cambodia.

A number of measures are currently under consideration by the Cambodian government. All crocodile farms must be registered and their animals marked using microchips. This would insure no farm is still receiving wild-caught animals, and any found doing so would be suspended. Support and training must also be provided to improve husbandry and productivity of the system. Increasing the supply of crocodiles from the animals currently in the farms may decrease the demand for those caught in the wild.

The Siamese Crocodile is listed under Appendix I of the Convention on International Trade in Endangered Species (CITES), the international treaty of which Cambodia is a signatory[51]. This provides the species with the strictest level of restrictions on international trade.

Vietnamese rice soup seller,
Kbal Taol, Pursat

The Cambodian government and its trading partners must use this tool effectively to properly control and manage all crocodile exports.

However, the future threat to Siamese Crocodiles in Cambodia may not be from exports, but imports. Hybrids, particularly between Siamese and Estuarine Crocodiles, but also Cuban Crocodiles, are appearing in a number of farms around the lake, with animals usually reported to have originated in Thailand. Thai farmers believe that hybrids are superior in both growth and reproductive potential and actively encourage hybridization. The situation is so extreme in Thailand that all Siamese Crocodiles in captivity have been genetically polluted to the point that they now have little conservation value.

Estuarine Crocodiles once occurred wild in the Tonle Sap, as evidenced by the recent discovery of an old jaw bone from the lake mud, but they are now long extinct[52]. Their return, through the introduction of hybrid animals to crocodile farms, greatly limits future conservation options for Siamese Crocodiles. This is not only due to the risk of escape, but also the genetic contamination of Siamese Crocodile stocks that could be used for future reintroduction. Without firm action Cambodia's crocodiles may be heading in the same direction as Thailand's.

Crocodiles aren't the only species whose modern introduction into the Tonle Sap ecosystem may bring about unforeseen consequences. At least two floating farms in Chong Kneas have in recent years raised Chinese Softshell Turtles for the food market. These turtles have now been found as wild-caught animals in local markets suggesting that as in other countries where they are farmed, they may be establishing populations in the wild[53]. Their potential affect on native turtle populations is unknown.

Golden Apple Snails were first brought from South America to Taiwan in 1980. Now farmed for food across Southeast Asia, they have escaped into natural

environments throughout the region. They were first reported from Cambodia in 1995, and are currently raised in at least nine provinces[54]. Recent studies show that invasions of Golden Apple Snails can result in an almost complete collapse of aquatic plant communities, leading to previously plant-dominated, clear water environments becoming turbid and algae dominated[55]. One species that may benefit from this, however, is the snail-eating specialist, the Asian Openbill stork. In central Thailand the burgeoning population of Golden Apple Snails is believed to have resulted in the greatly increasing numbers of Asian Openbills[56].

A recent study identified seventeen species of fish introduced into the Mekong basin that had either established populations or had the strong possibility of doing so[57]. However, they seem as yet to have had no significant adverse consequences and until now none appear to have become established in the Tonle Sap, perhaps due to the limited development of aquaculture around the lake[58]. One to watch, however, is the Red-throated Tilapia, one of the most widespread aquaculture fish in the region. African in origin, it was first introduced into Thailand in 1949 and is now present in Cambodia. It has escaped into the wild across the region, forming dense populations of stunted fish. Regarded as a pest, unsuccessful attempts to eliminate it have been made in many areas of the world.

Another potential concern could be the African Catfish, introduced into aquaculture systems in Vietnam in 1974. It has since been widely used for aquaculture across the region and has established itself in the wild throughout the Mekong basin. It has also been hybridized

with native catfish and there are reports that the hybrid may be responsible for a decline in the abundance of the native catfish *Clarias batrachus*. Both African Catfish and the hybrids are tolerant of poor water quality and de-oxygenated environments, giving them a competitive advantage over the native species[59].

However, the introduced species that are currently of most serious concern in the Tonle Sap ecosystem are the plants. More than a dozen exotic species can now be found around the lake, the worst two noxious invasives from South America: Water Hyacinth and Giant Mimosa.

Water Hyacinth is a floating weed with a remarkably high growth rate. On the Tonle Sap it forms dense mats clogging the slow-moving waterways, pools and back waters. It out-competes native aquatic species and de-oxygenates the water, reducing both water quality and fish production[60]. In the dry season it forms an almost impenetrable barrier to boat transportation, even making travel difficult along Prek Toal's 'high-street'. It is occasionally used for pig fodder, making *samras* – natural fish attracting devices and even handicrafts and hammocks. If it is to be effectively controlled, these uses, particularly animal fodder, should be encouraged.

More serious is the invasion of Giant Mimosa. An aggressive thorny shrub that grows several metres tall, it was first introduced to Thailand in 1947 as a green manure and a cover crop for tobacco. It was also planted along banks as it was thought that being prickly it would restrict access and therefore reduce erosion[61]. It now blankets large areas of wetlands and bank-sides throughout Thailand. It quickly forms dense, impenetrable thickets that choke out native plants. Evidence from Thailand indicates that it is disliked by native wildlife, particularly birds, and observations by Cambodian fishermen suggest that its affects on fish may be similar. No one knows when it reached Cambodia, but it is now found all along the Tonle Sap River, and at scattered locations around the shores of the lake, particularly in floating villages such as Chong Kneas, Chnouk Tru and Prek Toal[62].

The distribution of mimosa around the lake appears linked to human influence, as it is rarely found far from villages. Its aggressive nature means that it is among the first plants to re-colonise any disturbed area, such as cultivated land around villages. There are even indications from Vietnam that fire may actually trigger the germination process[63]. Plus, in both Australia and Thailand the dispersal of mimosa has been linked to the movement of domestic livestock and in Thailand road transportation has spread seeds along highways. Perhaps Cambodian villagers moving in and out of the Tonle Sap floodplain are inadvertently carrying mimosa with them?

Whilst the occurrence of mimosa remains localised around the Tonle Sap, appropriate actions can still be taken to curb the infestation. Tests in similar flood inundation systems of the Mekong Delta in Vietnam have shown that the most effective eradication method is to manually cut each stem as the flood rises. Stems were cut when the rising water was about 30cm deep, and when the water receded 75% to 90% had died[64]. Such eradication programs should begin in Cambodia before the process becomes so extensive as to be logistically impossible or prohibitively expensive.

**Map of settlements in and around the Tonle Sap inundation zone, naming some of the most important**

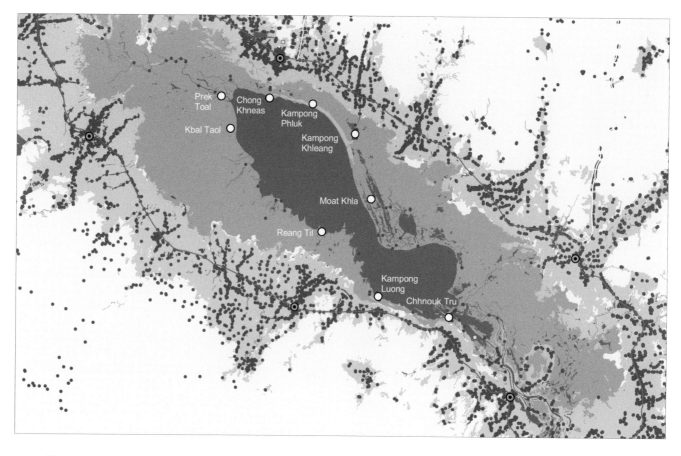

Prek Toal

Chong Khneas

Kampong Phluk

Kbal Taol

Kampong Khleang

Moat Khla

Reang Til

Kampong Luong

Chhnouk Tru

■ regular flood inundation zone

▨ wet rice farming

● settlements

○ major lake settlements

However, it may be too late, as current infrastructure development plans for the Tonle Sap will change the way of life for many lake communities, and may result in much larger numbers of people coming onto the floodplain. The Asian Development Bank (ADB) is now providing a multi-million dollar loan to the government for the development of a new port at Chong Kneas. The project will dredge a six kilometre canal from the lake to a permanent harbour basin at the foot of Phnom Kraom. The mud from the canal and harbour will be used to landfill an area of over 70 hectares adjacent to Phnom Kraom where the current inhabitants of the floating village will be resettled. The project is justified by the need to improve environmental conditions for the Chong Kneas community, but a coalition of NGOs have criticised it on the grounds that it will in fact accentuate environmental and social problems in the area[65].

In January 2005 reports indicated that the government had decided not to proceed with the project[66].

However, the following month the ADB endorsed its new five year strategy for Cambodia which emphasized development of the Tonle Sap basin[67]. Chong Kneas was always the first stage of an infrastructure program that potentially included the development of at least one other port on the lake at Chhnouk Tru, Kompong Chhnang[68].

The biggest problem facing not only Chong Kneas, but the future of the Tonle Sap, is the influx of immigrants such development projects would draw. Improving transportation and access to markets will create new opportunities and in turn lead to the creation of further infrastructure around the lake. Unregulated development will bring with it greater risk to the Tonle Sap ecosystem and therefore to the people living on it. The current floating village way of life may not be with us for much longer.

*Mimosa pigra* choking the
village waterways, Chong
Kneas, Siem Reap

# THE LAST CROCODILES

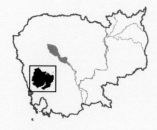

Depicted all over the walls of temples throughout Angkor, crocodiles have long had a significant role in Cambodian folklore. Although now verging on extinction in the Tonle Sap itself, Cambodia is still the last stronghold of the Siamese Crocodile. This decline is a result of years of persecution due to fear and ignorance (Siamese Crocodiles unlike some of their larger relatives are not known to attack humans) and the demand for crocodile skins for the lucrative leather trade. One of the world's rarest crocodilians, Siamese Crocodiles used to occur throughout Southeast Asia, but can now be found in the wild only in Cambodia and in small, probably unviable, pockets in Thailand, Laos and possibly Vietnam.

**Crocodile in the Churning of the Ocean of Milk, Angkor Wat east gallery**

They still occur throughout Cambodia but are now restricted to remote, wild areas, well away from people. Their stronghold is the rivers and wetlands of the Cardamom Mountains to the south of the Tonle Sap. These populations were discovered in early 2000 and are now the focus of a conservation program implemented by the Cambodian government in cooperation with Fauna and Flora International. The are currently thought to be at least 140 animals in 18 discrete localities across the Cardamoms, with the most important populations being in the marshes of Veal Veng and the Areng river valley[69]. Fortunately for the crocodiles, both these areas are inside the 420,000ha Central Cardamom Protected Forest, designated by the Cambodian government in 2002 and managed with the support of Conservation International.

The area of Veal Veng marsh is also home to a long-established community who have a traditional cultural respect for the crocodiles. They reportedly revere the animals and will not harm them, believing the death of a crocodile will bring bad luck. Unfortunately, as the area opens up to the rest of the country, newcomers do not hold the crocodiles in the same regard and they are becoming threatened by hunting. The conservation program is trying to build on the traditional belief systems and hiring local community members to protect the crocodiles.

Today one of the main threats to these animals is still the trade, as young animals are caught to supply crocodile farms. The success of conservation projects such as these is essential if the species is to survive in the wild. As with much of Cambodia's threatened wildlife, the country has plenty of remaining suitable habitat. So if areas can be effectively secured and animals protected from hunting for the long-term, crocodiles breed quickly and recovery of wild populations is possible.

Another long-term option may rest with the many Siamese Crocodiles held captive in the crocodile farms. Many of these animals may not have been held captive for that long, and assuming their genetic purity can be confirmed and secured, reintroduction into areas formerly inhabited may be possible. In this case, if all these parameters could be met, where better for a reintroduction program than the Prek Toal Core Area of the Tonle Sap? Crocodiles certainly used to occur in the area and returning animals would be protected by the lake's most effective team of conservation rangers. If such an initiative succeeded one day it may be possible to see crocodiles again, not only in the Great Lake, but perhaps, if people's fears could be overcome, also in the moat around Angkor Wat?

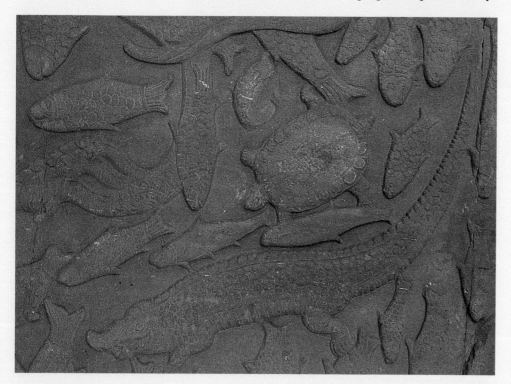

LEFT:
**Farmed crocodiles in a floating cage**

BELOW LEFT:
**The upper reaches of the Sre Ambel River, Koh Kong**

BELOW RIGHT:
**A rare of a wild Siamese Crocodile, Sre Ambel River, Koh Kong**
**©Allan Michaud**

# THE FISHING LOTS OF BATTAMBANG

In 1860, when French explorer Henri Mouhot crossed the Tonle Sap on his journey to Angkor, he wrote of the sheer numbers of fish hindering progress as they struck oars and the hull of the boat. The lake was, he commented, the centre of a huge fishing system that supported thousands if not millions of people[70]. Today, while at first glance the kilometres of bamboo fences and assorted fish traps may look primitive, they are incredibly effective fish-catching machines perfected over centuries to commercially exploit the lake on an industrial scale.

An estimated 1.2 million Cambodians living on the floodplain are employed in fisheries. They are one of the highest per capita consumers of fish in the world, with fish contributing an estimated 80% of dietary protein. In 2002 the total retail value of Cambodia's fish catch was estimated at over $300 million[71], while in the same year the total national Government expenditure on health was only $43 million[72]. Cambodia's freshwater fishery is critical to both the economy and food security – the health of the nation's heart and stomach.

Cambodia's current freshwater catch is estimated to be about 700,000 tonnes, globally the fourth greatest after three much larger countries: China, India and Bangladesh[73]. The Tonle Sap itself has an estimated yield per unit area that exceeds the floodplains of Bangladesh, Thailand or Indonesia, and is probably unrivalled as a fishery. The reason for this is the magnitude and timing of the flood. Every year as the rising water inundates the floodplain, fish have access to an extensive environment rich in nutrients. The dependability of the system has allowed fish to evolve to take maximum advantage of the enormous

A section of the hundreds of kilometres fish trap fence on the Tonle Sap, fishing lot #2, Battambang

Local villagers selling their catch at the end of the day to a fish trader, Prek Toal, Battambang

quantities of food produced by this annual opportunity.

It is not only one of most productive, but one of the most diverse fish systems in the world. According to a leading Mekong fish taxonomist, Walter Rainboth, more than 2,000 species occur in the Mekong system[74], and over 500 are recorded from Cambodia. In the Tonle Sap itself there are around 200 species of which more than 100 regularly occur in catches[75]. Per unit area, the Mekong has more fish species than the Amazon. This diversity is a product of the area's geological history and the great range of habitat types found within the system. The Mekong also has a number of endemics – species found nowhere else – although most of them are restricted to the upriver system. None of the species recorded from the Tonle Sap are endemic and most of them occur widely in the lower Mekong.

The fish of the Mekong have long been classified by fisheries biologists into two groups: 'white fish' and 'black fish', based upon their life cycles. The white fish, named as they spend a large proportion of their life in fast flowing 'white' water, are those that undertake annual, often lengthy, migrations synchronised with the flood cycle. These range in size from the small cyprinid, known in Khmer as *trey riel*, to the Mekong Giant Catfish. During the wet season they fatten themselves on the rich nutrients of the inundated floodplain, but as the water starts to drop they move back to deeper water, first into the lake before migrating on up the Mekong. They spend the dry season in deep pools in the river, sometimes as far upstream as southern Laos. Here they await the return of the flood. With the onset of the rainy season they spawn

Selling fish, Psa Kraom, Siem Reap

Catching migratory fish as they move out of the lake down the Tonle Sap River, Prek Phneou, Kandal

Selling snakehead fish, Psa Kraom, Siem Reap

and as the waters rise large numbers of eggs and larvae are carried downstream and swept onto the floodplain.

The black fish, species such as snakeheads, gouramis and catfish, migrate only short distances and live throughout the year on the surrounding floodplain. They spawn in the flooded scrub and swamps during high water and return to permanent ponds in the dry season. These fish are adapted to withstand drought conditions, such as the low levels of dissolved oxygen, found on the floodplain in the dry season. Some are able to breathe air and others are even capable of crossing dry land in search of water if their ponds dry up.

The fishery has evolved a complexity over the centuries to match the variety of fish species and strategies. The fisheries management system of Cambodia is one of the most developed anywhere in the world. The fisheries are organised legally into three levels: family (subsistence), medium-scale (artisanal) and large-scale (industrial). Family fishing for consumption is allowed year round, with restrictions only placed on equipment. Medium and large scale fisheries are permitted only during an open season which, in the Tonle Sap, stretches from November to June.

Around 200 types of fishing gear and methods have been recorded in the floodplain and rivers of Cambodia[76], and each has evolved for a specific role in a specific location. Gears range from simple basket traps, hooks and lines to large trawl, seine and lift nets. Much of this gear, such as basket traps are made from local materials: bamboo, rattan or vine. However, the most popular gear by far is now the monofilament gill-net.

The largest operations are the fishing lots. These vast fisheries are essentially large areas of the floodplain which the government rents out to private businessmen as concessions. This system has operated in Cambodia since the 19th century, but was formalised by the French colonial government in the fisheries law of 1908. It has always been, and remains, a lucrative way to generate both formal and non-formal tax revenues.

From the early 20th century until this day the management of lots has remained much the same. Every two years lots are sold off in a public auction to the highest bidder. The buyer purchases exclusive rights to exploit the fish in a defined area – during the open season – for the two-year period. Each lot owner is given a 'burden-book' which outlines the rules and regulations associated with the particular lot, for example what types of traps can be

Children fishing through the porch floor of a floating house, Prek Toal, Battambang

ABOVE:
**Making a bamboo fishing fence on a loom, Kompong Phluk, Siem Reap**

LEFT:
**Sewing a bamboo fishing fence, Kompong Phluk, Siem Reap**

FAR LEFT:
**Dip-net fishing at the mouth of the Sangke River, Prek Toal, Battambang**

placed where, or areas to be excluded from fishing for specific reasons. The burden book also confirms the obligation of the lot owner to protect the natural habitat within the lot boundaries.

Over the years the lot system has gradually decreased in size. In 1919 more than 14,000 square kilometres of the country were under fishing lots, but since then the area has been reduced by 70%[77]. However, the lots are still extensive, and on the Tonle Sap floodplain there are currently 39 totalling a little under 3,000 square kilometres. The largest, Lot # 2 in the swamp forest of Battambang, adjacent to Prek Toal village, is over 500 square kilometres. Historically, the lots have not only always comprised the largest, but also the most productive areas of the floodplain. Access to the best fishing has therefore long been limited to those few with the financial or political means to afford it.

Lot activities begin in November with the building of the boundary fences. Bamboo fences, kilometres long,

are constructed on shore and erected around the lot. They are built not simply to mark the boundaries and keep people out, but to keep the fish in. The lots work on the principle of trapping fish as they move to deeper water as the flood drops. In January or February, when the water has fallen to about four meters, fishing activity begins in earnest, and the fences start channelling the fish moving out of the swamp forest and floodplain into pens and traps. The catch is dominated by black fish, particularly Giant Snakeheads, one of the most valuable Tonle Sap species.

While this system of privatizing resources may be a sensible way to manage fisheries and maximize national revenues, especially in light of the government's lack of capacity, it has resulted in a history of problems. The first difficulty has long been the way in which lots are allocated. While publicly the process is an auction, allegedly many purchasers have in fact secured their investments well beforehand through 'under the table' payments. This

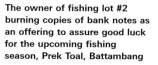

The owner of fishing lot #2 burning copies of bank notes as an offering to assure good luck for the upcoming fishing season, Prek Toal, Battambang

lack of transparency results in a public under-valuation of the lots and greater financial benefits ending up in the hands of the already wealthy rather than the state[78].

The problem has been exacerbated by the sale of what are termed 'research lots', which have included a majority of the most valuable lots. These lots are taken out of the auction process, supposedly to be managed for research into fisheries and habitat management, for up to six years at a time. In reality, little or no research is conducted and most are simply operated on a commercial basis in the same way as conventional lots. The difference is that the sale of research lots is done in secret, leading to allegations that many end up in the hands of influential politicians and rich businessmen[79].

Having acquired a lot, the owner sets about protecting his investment. All lot-owners traditionally hire armed security guards drawn from the ranks of the police or military. The major function of these guards is to prevent unauthorised access to the lot. This has the positive affect of protecting not only the fish but also all the other resources within the concession, particularly the swamp forest. However, it has also led to regular conflicts over access, even with people simply travelling across a lot between local communities. Villagers living around lots often complain that they face intimidation and harassment. Unfortunately, shooting incidents involving lot guards, sometimes with fatal consequence, are not uncommon[80].

The highest yielding fishery on the Tonle Sap is actually small-scale family fishing. Despite being restricted to small, single-operated gear such as cast-nets, single long lines and small dip-nets, these fishermen produce a greater total catch than that of the lots. However, family fishermen complain that they can no longer catch enough fish for their needs, and that the size and power of the lots restrict their access to productive fishing areas. Instead family fishermen are now resorting to more effective, but illegal, gear – primarily small-mesh, monofilament gillnets. These modern nylon nets set in the water are indiscriminate and catch even the youngest fish. In some areas, the situation is such that any fish that escapes being caught in the lot is highly likely to be caught by a gill-net.

During the wet season of July, August and September, when the lots are gone and there is open access to the swamp forest, these nylon gill-nets have given many family fishermen the opportunity to turn to catching water-snakes. The Tonle Sap is known to support seven species

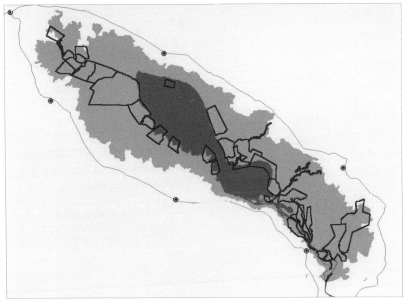

TOP:
**Egrets, herons and two Spot-billed Pelicans at a fish fence trap, Prek Toal, Battambang**

ABOVE:
**Map showing the current location of fishing lots (outlined in dark blue) in the flood inundation zone around the Tonle Sap lake**

of watersnake, of which five are harvested on a significant scale. Data gathered during 1999 estimated that a minimum of 8,500 watersnakes per day were caught and sold at the peak of the flood. These are caught as food or to feed crocodiles in farms around the lake. In addition, some are exported both live and as skins to Thailand, Vietnam and especially China. This is thought to represent the greatest single harvest of snakes anywhere in the world[81].

Commercial-scale harvesting of watersnakes is a recent phenomenon having begun only in the last decade. The reasons for the current level of the harvest appear to be threefold. Firstly the growing importance of the crocodile farming industry on the lake has created a novel and increased demand for a cheap food resource for the crocodiles. Secondly, watersnakes are caught exclusively using monofilament gill nets set semi-permanently in the swamp forest. Prior to the early 1990s these nets weren't widely available in Cambodia as they are today and this has

allowed fishermen access to a new resource.

Finally, as local villagers find fish harder to come by, particularly during high water, watersnakes become an alternative open access resource. Unlike fisheries, the watersnake harvest is totally unregulated and little is known about its sustainability. Research is ongoing to examine both the reproductive biology of these snakes and the exploitation levels. It may well be that management measures of some sort will soon be necessary to reduce the catch to sustainable levels.

There is little historical information on the sustainability of fish catches in Cambodia, but a growing human population has led to increased fishing pressure, and the catches of individual fishermen have undoubtedly decreased. Significant declines are also known to have taken place in some of the larger species, particularly those that spawn later in life. The longer a species takes to mature, the more vulnerable it becomes to over-fishing. Although no species is yet known to have gone extinct in the Mekong system, some, such as the Mekong Giant Catfish, are now coming close[82, 83].

Catches are currently dominated by small, short-lived, rapidly reproducing species; a good example is the cyprinid *trey riel* which spawns after only one year. The resulting shift to a catch dominated by fish of smaller sizes has lead to a reduction in the average value of the fish catch per kilogramme. However, the overall catch is still thought to be increasing and some fisheries biologists have speculated that most smaller species are not yet over-fished and increasing fishing pressure may result in the catch increasing even further[84, 85]. More ominously though, even while the total catch may still increase there are indications that the average size of the dominant small fish such as *trey riel* is decreasing. This could well be the first sign of excessive fishing pressure on these stocks as well[86].

A number of issues underlie these changes and threaten the long term future of the Tonle Sap fishery. At a local level some of the most immediate are a range of

ABOVE:
**Repairing a fish trap being, Prek Toal, Battambang**

LEFT:
**Soldiers employed by the lot owner guarding the transfer of fish on the Tonle Sap in 1997, Battambang**

A local villager family fishing outside the lot with a hand dip-net, Battambang

unsustainable, and invariably illegal, fishing practises. As Cambodia is still recovering from years of war, explosives such as grenades have long been readily available. Their use, to catch fish in deep pools and spawning areas along the Mekong, has had a decimating effect on the reproductive success of many species that migrate to and from the Tonle Sap. In addition, not only do explosives kill indiscriminately, they can also destroy surrounding habitats. However, an increasing government emphasis on demobilising and disarming the over-sized military and a growing awareness of the negative effects of explosive fishing is now having a positive affect.

In addition to the increasing use of small-mesh gill-nets, there is growing concern over two other fishing methods on the increase with access to new technologies. While all methods of pumping, bailing and draining are illegal they are commonly practiced. Historically, local fishermen bailing water from ponds by hand was not seen as a particularly significant issue. However, the availability of small powerful pumps, primarily designed for irrigation, has changed this. Now the total draining of fish refuges is a quick and easy job, catching not only all the fish, but destroying an ecosystem in the process. It is of particular concern in swamp forest fishing lots where productive streams are dammed and then pumped dry.

The use of electro-fishing gears is also on the increase. Previously this was of little concern as the necessary equipment was cumbersome, comparatively expensive and not easily available. However, portable car batteries are now cheap and straightforward to both acquire and recharge, even in rural areas. Easy to carry and very

effective, they not only kill fish but everything else within range. Concerned by this the government is attempting to crack down on the growing use of this illegal equipment.

One species of major conservation concern is the pangasius river catfish. These fish have been raised for centuries on the Mekong floodplain as a highly-valued food fish. It is the dominant species raised in the pen and cage culture on the Tonle Sap. However, the stocking of these culture systems is based almost entirely on wild-caught young fingerling or fry, known in Khmer as *pra*. Despite being banned in 1994, collection of wild catfish fry for culture is extensive across Cambodia.

There is also a flourishing illegal international trade in fry to Vietnam to meet the demand of catfish farmers in the Mekong Delta. In Vietnam the fish are matured and many end up in the export market. In 1998 an estimated 1-2 billion fry were caught in Cambodia[87], most of which were reportedly smuggled by boat to Vietnam in individual shipments of 5-10 million fry[88]. The demand is exacerbated by the belief that wild caught fry is better and therefore fetches a higher price.

River catfish are late-in-life spawners with sexual maturation taking more than three years. Because of increasing fishing pressure only a small percentage of fish now reach spawning age. Evidence suggests that river catfish have greatly declined, and present rates of exploitation are intense for fish of all ages. The fry fishery, often carried out using very small-mesh gill-nets or even mosquito nets, also has a negative effect on other species caught as unwanted by-catch. If this illegal and destructive fishery is

**Catching watersnakes during the wet season, Prek Toal Core Area, Battambang**

to be controlled before the wild stock is completely exhausted, aquaculture initiatives focusing on native species must be encouraged and the availability of hatchery produced fry must be increased.

In response to all these problems the government has initiated a number of policies to curb over-exploitation and allow local people greater access to the fishery resource. This culminated on 24 October 2000 with Prime Minister Hun Sen reducing the fishing lot areas by 56 per cent, or over 5,000 square kilometres. The areas released were turned over to community fishing. The hope is that extensive areas previously exploited using 'regulated' large-scale commercial gear will now be fished entirely by family fishermen with small-scale gear. However, the lack of legal structures and the fact that few have any real understanding of community fisheries management has lead to confusion over access rights and allegations of uncontrolled exploitation and increased illegal fishing.

Challenges to effective fisheries co-management are great. Cambodian villages lack community structure or organized groupings above the family level. Since the time of Angkor the feudal nature of Khmer society has meant that 'communities' are political administrative units rather

**Sunset on the Tonle Sap, Prek Preah Kantiel, Battambang**

than social entities. Today the system of patronage between peasants and authority continues, and power rests with government officers, particularly the police or military. On top of this traditional hierarchy came the trauma and displacement of the Khmer Rouge years and long-running ethnic divisions with most of the fishing skills resting primarily with Vietnamese and Cham[89]. Hopes that traditional theories of community management, where individuals work for a collective benefit, will be appropriate in rural Cambodia are largely misplaced.

Over the past decade foreign donors, who prop up the majority of the national budget and aim to better the lives of everyday Cambodians, have paid far too much attention to the demise of Cambodia's forests. Pushed by lobbies in Europe, where images of tropical deforestation sell better than those of a threatened fishery, they have neglected the country's fish stocks. Yet it is the fish of the Tonle Sap, not the forests of the Cardamom Mountains, on which the lives of Cambodians depend. What is needed is renewed donor interest and investment in the fisheries sector. Experimentation with co-management should continue, but alongside other management strategies. A new fisheries law is in the process of being passed, but the real challenge will be in enforcement. There must be transparency in the fishing lot system, with any remaining research lots really being used for research. The lots themselves if properly managed could protect the resources well, but the short duration of their tenure promotes over-exploitation. The concession period could be increased to encourage owners to take a longer term perspective on fish and habitat management.

Genuine fish sanctuaries need to be established in key areas not only to conserve fish stocks but for the health of the whole ecosystem. Research into the sustainability of the catch and potential management interventions should continue, as should research into native species in aquaculture, especially in areas away from the floodplain. The true worth of Cambodia's fisheries must be properly recognised across all sectors, not only agricultural development and the value of swamp forest conservation, but in ministries concerned with industrial development, transport, power and finance.

# AN UNDERWATER WORLD OF GIANTS

At three metres long and 300kg, the Mekong Giant Catfish is one of the largest freshwater fish anywhere to be found. And it's not just catfish that grow to such gigantic proportions in the fertile waters of the Mekong and the Tonle Sap. There is the four metre by two metre Giant Stingray and the 100kg Giant Barb. All of these fish exist nowhere else, but are today not only some of the largest, but unfortunately some of the most endangered fish in the world.

Known as the 'King of fish' in Cambodia, the Mekong Giant Catfish has long been revered by commu-nities along the river. Historically it was found up the Mekong as far as China, but American biologist Zeb Hogan estimates it has declined by as much as 90% in just the past two decades. On the Mekong in northern Thailand, where an individual fish could sell for up to $4,000, it has all but disappeared. It may well now be extinct as a wild fish in the upper Mekong.

Concerned by this decline, Hogan began working with the Cambodian Department of Fisheries to initiate a research program on the species. The Mekong Giant Catfish has never been popular as an eating fish in

**Releasing a Mekong Giant Catfish on the Tonle Sap River north of Phnom Penh**

LEFT:
**Zeb Hogan and colleagues
measuring a catfish**

BELOW:
**Dead Mekong Giant Catfish,
Chroy Chongvar, Phnom Penh**

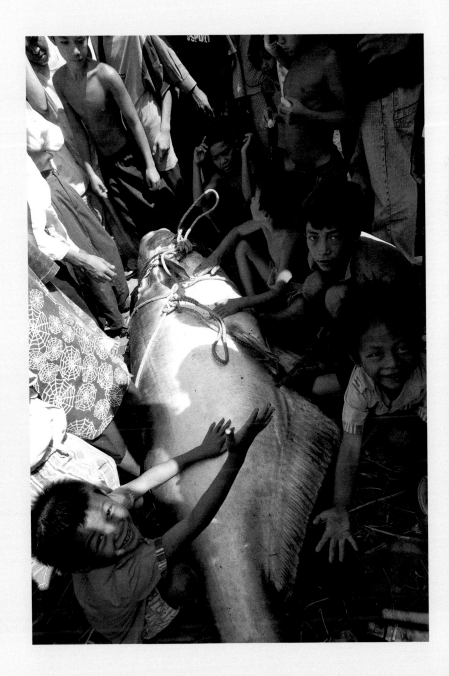

Cambodia and still survives in the Tonle Sap and main-stream Mekong. Every year small numbers are regularly reported caught as they migrate out of the Tone Sap. The research team worked with local fishermen offering them a reward equivalent to the local market price (about 50 cents per kg), for every Mekong Giant Catfish reported. They then released the fish alive with the addition of a unique plastic tag and an acoustic transmitter.

The success of this approach has resulted, over four years, in the purchase, tagging and release of 21 Mekong Giant Catfish, primarily from the migratory fish traps on the Tonle Sap River close to Phnom Penh. This has now become a part of a much larger government research program working with ten other vulnerable fish species, including the other giants – barb and stingray. As a result of this initiative, 5,000 fish have now been bought, marked and are swimming free again. From this scheme much is being learnt about the migration patterns and therefore the conservation of these species.

As yet there have been no reports of any of the tagged Mekong Giant Catfish, but there is now proof that other catfish species migrate out of the Tonle Sap and up the Mekong River north of Kratie, probably to spawn. Evidence suggests that Mekong Giant Catfish do likewise and spend the dry season in deep pools amongst the Mekong rapids, perhaps even travelling as far as Thailand[90].

Even if it maybe already too late to save the Mekong Giant Catfish, the hope is that the increasing knowledge and awareness that this program is generating will help save other species of the Mekong's unique, if not so giant, fish.

# PREK TOAL: THE CORE AREAS OF THE BIOSPHERE RESERVE

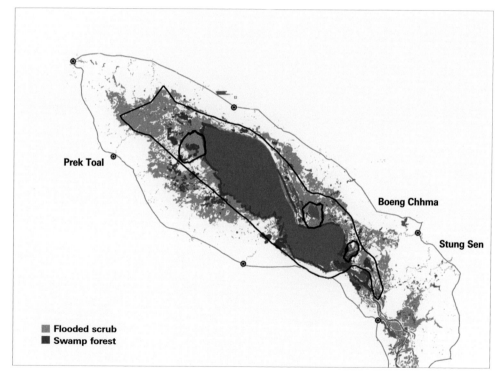

ABOVE:
**Map showing the extent of flooded scrub and swamp forest habitat around the Tonle Sap and the boundaries of the Biosphere Reserve and the three Core Areas**

OPPOSITE:
**Travelling through the Prek Toal Core Area in the wet season**

The short 45 minute boat trip across the Tonle Sap from Chong Kneas into the swamp forest to the south of Prek Toal is equivalent to a long journey back in time. The Prek Toal Core Area of the Tonle Sap Biosphere Reserve, is one of the last undisturbed areas on the lake, and probably the closest that is left to what the Tonle Sap may have looked like long before Angkor.

In October 1997 UNESCO accepted the nomination of the Tonle Sap into the global network of Biosphere Reserves. Three core areas were proposed: Prek Toal, Boeung Chhma and Stung Sen. Finally, in April 2001, these were designated under Cambodian law by a Royal Decree. This states that the core zones are "devoted to the long term protection and conservation of natural resources and the ecosystem", specifically "to preserve flooded forest, fish, wildlife, hydrological systems and natural beauty."

Going into the Prek Toal Core Area at any time feels much like entering a coastal mangrove forest, whether floating amongst crowns of submerged trees during the 'high tide' wet season, or struggling through knee-deep mud and impenetrable vegetation at 'low tide' dry season. The true swamp forest south of Prek Toal is a mosaic of mature stands – between seven and fifteen metres tall, dense thorny bushes and more open areas. Species poor, it is dominated by just two tree species and a number of vines and climbing lianas. Palms, with the exception of some rattans, are completely absent as are ephiphytes and – unlike mangroves – any trees with aerial roots.

Most of the trees and shrubs of the swamp forests are deciduous. However, they lose their leaves not in the

**The wet season swamp forest of the Prek Toal Core Area**

dry season, but during the flood when they are completely submerged. At a time most trees in Cambodia are experiencing their greatest growth period, those in the swamp forest of Prek Toal are under several metres of water and shedding their leaves in response to maximum stress. Certain species will on occasion keep their leaves through the wet season and continue to photosynthesise underwater. As soon as the flood recedes all the trees undergo a rapid growth of new leaves, with flowering and fruiting peaking from June-August. By the time the lake floods again the trees are laden with fruits and seeds to be dispersed by the rising water, and, possibly as importantly, by fish. The latter is still conjecture, but in the crystal clear flood waters of the swamp forest, fruits certainly make an easily visible passing meal.

Despite the fact that the system is relatively low in species diversity, a large number of the trees are endemic to Cambodia and several to the Mekong floodplain or the Tonle Sap itself. The similarity to mangrove is far from superficial. For instance the endangered, endemic tree species *Terminalia cambodiana*, or *taour* in Khmer, is found only in the Tonle Sap and Cambodia's coastal mangroves. These elements indicate that in geological time the lake

has been more recently influenced by the sea than other river systems.

The mature swamp forest of the Prek Toal Core Area is now limited to the more intensively flooded parts of the lake along permanent water courses and the dry season fringe. Originally forest such as this would have been found across the Cambodian floodplain, but the factors governing just how extensive this was are unclear. Humans have had a long and significant impact on the vegetation of the floodplain. Cutting for fuelwood and timber, and burning for clearing or hunting has impacted the forest for centuries and these activities have accelerated markedly over the past decade. Today high levels of disturbance mean that vegetation around the lake is in a constant state of degradation and regeneration. However, a pattern is discernible with the largest tress and true swamp forest occurring only where there is perpetual water; moving inland trees become more stunted leading eventually to domination by grasses and scrub. It has been suggested that these dryer areas have never supported large trees as they do not contain enough moisture.

In the 19th century Henri Mouhot[91] described the shore of the Tonle Sap as "thickly covered with trees which are half submerged". Villagers living in lake-edge communities today, claim that within living memory many areas of scrub were formerly forested. Such evidence indicates that human factors must have had a significant influence on the vegetation. Perhaps the wetter, more inundated, parts of the floodplain where the true swamp forest is found are less vulnerable to fire and therefore the larger trees have survived?

What is certain is that the total area of the floodplain under forest cover has decreased significantly. The mature swamp forest remaining in the three core zones now represents the last significant example of this ecosystem not just on the Tonle Sap, but anywhere in Asia. The exact rate of decline, even over the last fifty years, is difficult to calculate, primarily due to the different forest classification systems used over the years. However, based on the broadest arrangement of forest types, including scrub and patchy trees, the total has shrunk from more than one million hectares during the 1930s, to 614,000ha in the late 1960s and 360,000ha by the 1990s[92].

A key factor in decreasing swamp forest has been its conversion to agriculture for rice production. However, there has also long been commercial exploitation of the flood plain for both firewood and charcoal. It is estimated

LEFT:
**Tree crowns emerging from the flood water in the wet season, Prek Toal Core Area**

BELOW LEFT:
**The clear water of the swamp forest in the wet season, Prek Toal Core Area**

**Catching fish by hand in the swamp forest in the dry season**

Burning and clearing swamp
forest for conversion to rice
fields, Siem Reap

than during the French colonial administration in the early part of the 20th century the Tonle Sap produced 85% of Cambodia's firewood and charcoal[93]. Such activities still continue at a local level across the floodplain, and are of particular concern in the outer perimeter, preventing any effective regeneration.

The situation in the core zone is somewhat different. Most wood-cutting in these areas occurs during the flood. At this season access is easier and exposed branches can be cut by hand and taken out by boat. Many of the swamp forest trees and shrubs appear remarkably resilient to this level of disturbance. Growth rates of up to two metres in a single season have been recorded following heavy cutting, and large trees cut in this way appear to regenerate their canopy so well they can be cut again in two or three years[94]. Without major commercial exploitation, and as long as cutting is not followed by burning, the swamp forest could probably supply local communities with a continued sustainable source of fuel. Unfortunately as the human population increases so do levels of exploitation and the resource base continues to dwindle.

In view of all the increasing pressures, why has the Prek Toal Core Area survived? The answer is not in the Biosphere Reserve and its protected status, but that it lies within some of the lake's most important fishing lots. Much as forest concession owners guard their investments, some visionary lot owners have protected the forest within their lot. The relationship is not quite so direct, but the function of swamp forest as a critical fish breeding and feeding habitat is now widely acknowledged. Data suggest that fishery productivity is directly related to the extent and quality of the forest. It is no coincidence that Battambang Lot #2, which contains the majority of the core zone, is also the most productive fishing lot on the Tonle Sap.

The healthy forest and fish populations are part of a system supporting a whole range of rare and unusual animals and birds. Fish-eating otters are one of the important mammal groups found around the lake. Two species, Smooth Otter and Hairy-nosed Otter, are known to occur in the swamp forest. The latter is little known and the Tonle Sap may represent its major stronghold worldwide. Nowadays, however, they are rarely seen as the demand for skins for traditional Cambodian medicine means all otters are heavily hunted.

Three primates, Slow Loris, Long-tailed Macaque and Silvered Langur, are found in the forest. How the

Cutting branches for firewood from the swamp forest

lorises cope during the flood is unknown, but both macaques and langurs happily take to the water and can be seen swimming between the tree crowns. Macaques are now being trapped in large numbers all around the lake in response to the recent demand from 'monkey farms', primarily in Vietnam, established to supply overseas pharmaceutical companies.

Flying-foxes or fruit bats also occur, forming large communal roosts in the swamp forest trees, sometimes amongst waterbird colonies. Precisely why they should mix in this way is not understood, but it may provide them with greater security. The flying-foxes are important pollinators and seed dispersers for a number of trees, although how these functions are carried out in the swamp forest remains unclear. Unfortunately flying-foxes too are declining, since wherever they are found across the country they are caught for the local restaurant trade.

The real global biodiversity value of the Tonle Sap, particularly Prek Toal, lies in its colonies of waterbirds. They are the largest and most important breeding grounds of storks, pelicans, ibises, cormorants and darters in Southeast Asia, both because of their size and the survival of several internationally important species.

ABOVE:
**Confiscated Long-tailed
Macaque, Forestry Office,
Siem Reap**

RIGHT:
**Employees of fishing lot #1 who
live temporarily inside the forest
during the fishing season,
Prek Tvang, Battambang**

Seventeen bird species classified as globally threatened or near-threatened find refuge around the Tonle Sap. Nine of these rely upon the swamp forest of the Prek Toal Core Area. Of greatest significance are the numbers of Spot-billed Pelican and Greater Adjutant. For these two, the birds at Prek Toal probably represent the single largest populations left anywhere in the world.

The importance of the birds of the Tonle Sap and the threats to them were little known until the 1990s when ornithologists returned for the first time since the early 1960s. Initial aerial surveys undertaken in 1992 brought back exciting stories of extensive colonies of large waterbirds south of Prek Toal. However, a follow-up visit to the villages by boat in 1994 yielded frightening news. In a single day researchers saw hundreds of stork chicks being raised for food on the porches of floating houses[95]. It was immediately clear that bird collection posed a serious threat to their survival.

In 1996 a joint Cambodian government-international team sponsored by IUCN worked in Prek Toal village during the breeding season. They estimated that 26,000 eggs and close to 3,000 chicks were harvested and sold for food that year. The eggs came predominantly from the nests of Spot-billed Pelican, Black-headed Ibis, Asian Openbill and Painted Stork, while the harvested chicks were almost exclusively Painted Storks[96]. The sheer scale of collection demonstrated that the levels of harvest were unsustainable and that this was the single most critical threat to the future of these birds.

The following year, another joint NGO-government team spent three months in Prek Toal during the breeding season. In an effort to better understand and try to prevent egg and chick collection they undertook socio-economic surveys in villages around the colonies. They discovered that birds gathered to breed in January as the water level dropped exposing the trees and young birds

**The water bird colonies of the Prek Toal Core Area from the air, each white tree represents a group of nesting birds that have stained the tree with their guano**

TOP:
**Nesting Spot-billed Pelicans, Prek Toal Core Area**

ABOVE:
**Colony of Darter and cormorants, Prek Toal Core Area**

TOP:
**Nesting Spot-billed Pelicans and a Greater Adjutant, Prek Toal Core Area**

ABOVE:
**Nesting Little and Indian Cormorants, Prek Toal Core Area**

hatched in February and March. At this time the chicks were collected from the nest and brought back to the village. Here they were fattened for eating at the Cambodian New Year in mid-April, much like people in the west would eat turkey at Christmas or Thanksgiving.

The job of the waterbird harvester was extremely arduous involving long periods of time deep in the almost impenetrable forest. It was one of the least desired jobs and left to the poorest of the community. As the villages floated upon one of the most productive fisheries in the world, the birds were not a key protein source and bird collection was only a livelihood issue for a small number of villagers[97]. The work of the team increased the awareness of both villagers and local authorities of the seriousness and importance of the issue, and led to a significant reduction in collection that year. In Koh Chivang Commune, one of their main focal villages, no birds were harvested after February 18th that year.

However, despite this, egg collecting continued in the seasons that followed with recurrent arrests of poachers. In response to this a local conservation team was initiated to protect the colonies. By the breeding season of 2001, WCS working with the Government had hired

ABOVE LEFT:
**Ranger with a dying Great Cormorant, Prek Toal Core Area**

ABOVE:
**Captive young Grey Herons, Prek Toal, Battambang**

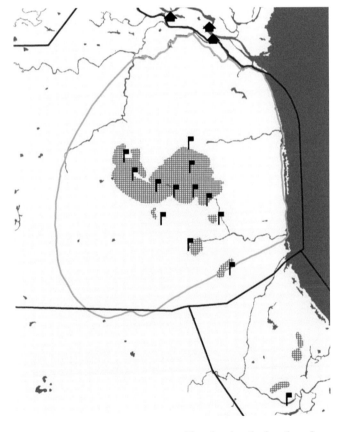

 Boundary of Core Area
Boundary of fishing lots
Waterbird Colonies
Prek Toal village
Ranger observation platforms

**Map showing the location of the waterbird colonies and ranger observation platforms within the boundary of the Prek Toal Core Area and Battambang fishing lot #2**

25 local villagers as rangers, 50% of whom were former bird collectors. Rangers are paid salaries and stationed on tree platforms to guard the colonies twenty four hours a day throughout the breeding season. They are trained not only to carry enforcement and awareness, but also to undertake regular bird counts to monitor the colonies.

The village ranger program has been extremely successful and although occasional cases of egg collection have occurred, the rate was down to three cases in 2002 and only one case in 2003. Alongside the protection work, Osmose, a Siem Reap-based NGO, runs an education project targeted at local schoolchildren. Not only do environmental educators now work in the village schools but every week the children are involved in activities with the rangers. Some weeks they draw pictures of birds to

make 'no entry' signs, in others they join bird counts. These activities both spread the conservation message across generations and create pride among rangers and villagers. Fathers, who were formerly bird collectors, are now able to gain new esteem from involving their children in their work.

The monitoring program has shown the results of this initiative to be startling. Prek Toal waterbird populations are rebounding. Darter, for which the data is most complete, have increased from less than 300 nests in 2000/2001 to more than 1,800 in 2004/2005. Similar things maybe happening with Spot-billed Pelicans and other species, but more data is needed. As important as the progress made on the ground is the fact that the team is now run and managed by Cambodians. The project represents one of the greatest conservation success stories not just in Cambodia, but across Southeast Asia.

The increasing bird numbers have brought with them benefits, but also potential problems. As the area is not only a 'protected' core zone, but also a commercial fishing lot there are concerns that more birds, particularly pelicans and cormorants, may result in less fish. The relationship between waterbirds and fisheries is complicated and not fully understood in any part of the tropical world. Most birds are selective in both the size and species of the fish they take, but, even basic knowledge of which those species are and whether they are commercially important is lacking. In Prek Toal there is no data to indicate that fish stocks are suffering, but the perception remains.

In defence of the birds, most fish breed during the flood, and therefore the time when fish fingerlings are at the greatest risk of predation is when the majority of birds

ABOVE:
**Prek Toal rangers working within the Prek Toal Core Area with Sun Visal (right of picture) of WCS**

TOP:
**Local police and rangers in Prek Toal with a boat full of heron and egret eggs confiscated from collectors arrested in 2003**

FAR LEFT:
Local school children in Prek Toal learning about the birds of the surrounding area in a class run by Osmose

LEFT:
A young child looking at the first ever Cambodian language bird book, Siem Reap

have dispersed, often hundreds of kilometres from Prek Toal. Plus, through their excrement, the birds are believed to benefit fisheries in a positive way, increasing productivity by returning huge amounts of nutrients to the ecosystem.

The waterbird colonies have also brought an unprecedented level of outside investment to Prek Toal. NGOs and international donors have now been supporting activities in the community and employing villagers for several years. This has not only been in the conservation field, but also in fisheries, education and health. Today Prek Toal is one of the most affluent floating communities on the Tonle Sap with a new health centre, school and pagoda. Finally, after years of seeing aid workers and conservationists, the villagers are welcoming a new type of moneyed foreigner, tourists.

'Ecotourism' represents a great hope, but also a great threat, to the future of the Prek Toal Core Area. In a country like Cambodia, it is often offered as the solution to a myriad of conservation problems. The belief is that wealthy foreign tourists with a desire to see wildlife and an untouched environment will provide long-term financial incentives to prevent short-term exploitation. In principle this sounds great, in practice in Cambodia, as in many developing countries, it is very difficult.

In the context of Prek Toal, how to ensure that the poorest – the former bird collectors – benefit most? If bird collectors don't benefit, why should they stop hunting? However, those who gain first from the tourists are the shop keepers, restaurateurs and boat owners, already some of the wealthiest in the community. In situations where levels of governance are often poor, how to be certain that

Prek Toal school children on an Osmose visit to the colonies watching birds from one of the ranger observation platforms

Darter colony, Prek Toal Core Area. The partially white birds are nestlings.

taxes on tourists do not end up in the wrong pockets? And in many areas of Cambodia, will foreign tourists ever generate sufficient income for ecotourism to be a viable alternative to logging?

If ecotourism can work anywhere in Cambodia, it is in Prek Toal. Just a short boat trip across the Tonle Sap from Angkor, hundreds of thousands of tourists a year are only a day's excursion away from one of the world's most important waterbird colonies. During December and January, the peak tourist season, the colonies are easily accessible and represent an intense wildlife experience.

Within the local community, the success of the conservation project to date provides a great foundation. Bird collectors turned conservation rangers are now being trained as guides. They may not be able to speak foreign languages, but who better to lead people through the maze of the swamp forest? And which villagers know more about the birds than those who used to live in the forest hunting them? This project brings together government and NGOs, who not only provide technical assistance but help ensure transparency. It also works within the community, integrating conservation, education and ecotourism.

There is real potential for a tourism boom in Prek Toal but conservation management systems are urgently required. Regulations need to define quotas for the number of boats and tourists, strict no-access zones that change with the season and the locations of specific colonies, designated access routes for boats and appropriate observation sites. Without these minimum requirements, tourists risk inadvertently disturbing and destroying the very thing they are coming to see.

If tourism is to provide a realistic future alternative to current resource extraction in the Prek Toal Core Area, then institutional changes are also needed. One of the greatest problems is the over-lapping responsibilities of agencies. Is the area to be managed for commercial fishing or biodiversity protection? Already this conflict is creating problems. Ministry of Environment staff charged with protecting the core zone can be forbidden access by the lot owner. In the long term, commercial fishing as currently practiced, is not compatible with the protection of biodiversity. Management of the core areas needs to become better integrated between the relevant government agencies, with the agreed objective of implementing the Biosphere Reserve as laid out in the Royal Decree.

The best way forward would be to designate the Prek Toal Core Area under the fisheries law as a fish sanctuary rather than a fishing lot. This is not only in line with Biosphere Reserve and core zone regulations, but by conserving the swamp forest would help secure the future of the fisheries throughout the Tonle Sap. Once effectively protected for conservation with appropriate management systems in place, the long term future of Prek Toal, its birds and fish, could all be paid for by tourist dollars.

ABOVE LEFT:
**Birdwatching tourists visiting the Prek Toal Core Area**

ABOVE:
**Darters with nestlings, Prek Toal Core Area**

## THE KING'S TURTLE

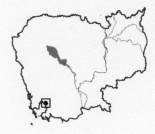

In the late 19th century when French geographer Auguste Pavie was exploring a remote river in southern Cambodia, he came across reports of nesting turtles whose eggs were collected solely for the consumption of the royal family. Over 100 years later, at the start of the 21st century, a team of Cambodian and US biologists found a small nesting population of Mangrove Terrapin – now one of the world's rarest turtles – in the Sre Ambel River, the very same river system travelled by Pavie. Locals in upriver communities even called the turtle by an old Khmer name literally translated as 'Royal turtle'. These were the very animals Pavie described all those years previously[98].

Ichthyologist Tyson Roberts has even speculated on another royal Cambodian link to Mangrove Terrapins, proposing that one or two of the turtles depicted in the bas reliefs of the Bayon at Angkor, might be Mangrove Terrapins[99]. The resemblance is perhaps superficial, but the mangrove-like swamp forest would be excellent habitat for Mangrove Terrapins, and they certainly used to occur in the Tonle Sap. In 1985, the shells of two adults were found buried in the mud of the lake. They are now in the Siem Reap Fisheries Office, but are not of recent origin and are thought to be at least 50 years old. Recent surveys have found no evidence of their persistence and the Mangrove Terrapin has now been added to the list of species lost from the Tonle Sap during the 20th century.

In southern Cambodia, near the town of Sre Ambel, a government project is now working to keep the country's Mangrove Terrapins alive in the 21st century. Department of Fisheries turtle conservation biologist Heng Sovannara works with WCS coordinating a team of villagers to protect the turtles. Along similar lines to the conservation rangers at Prek Toal, Sovannara has hired those people who used to collect turtle eggs and turned them into nest guards. They make sure that adult turtles are allowed to reach the nesting beaches and lay their eggs in peace, then protect the nest from predators or poachers until the eggs hatch.

The population is extremely small, with perhaps less than ten adult females surviving. However, in three years local school children and dignitaries have already participated in ceremonies releasing 130 young turtles back into the river. Mangrove Terrapins take a long time to mature and these young turtles will have to escape both hunters and being accidentally trapped in fishing gears for another twenty years before they themselves can breed. Exactly how far they will range during these years is still a mystery so the team is now taking up patrolling throughout the river system to protect these animals and raise awareness of their plight.

Mangrove Terrapin conservation is therefore a long-term investment, but the hope is that with the continued commitment of Sovannara and his team, and a bit of luck, the 'Royal turtles' of Sre Ambel won't follow those of the Tonle Sap, and will remain a part of Cambodia's heritage into the 22nd century.

**Heng Sovannara with a confiscated Mangrove Terrapin before it is released back to the river, Sre Ambel, Koh Kong**

LEFT:
**Working with local children to teach them about the Mangrove Terrapin, Sre Ambel, Koh Kong**

BELOW LEFT:
**Heng Sovannara showing Mangrove Terrapin tracks, indicating where a female had come the previous night to lay eggs, Sre Ambel, Koh Kong**

BELOW:
**Nao Thouk, Director of the Cambodian Fisheries Department with an old Mangrove Terrapin shell recovered from the mud of the Tonle Sap, Siem Reap**

BELOW:
**Protected Mangrove Terrapin nests on the Sre Ambel River, Koh Kong**

BOTTOM:
**A ranger at work guarding the turtle nesting beaches, Sre Ambel, Koh Kong**

# THE TONLE SAP RIVER AND PHNOM PENH

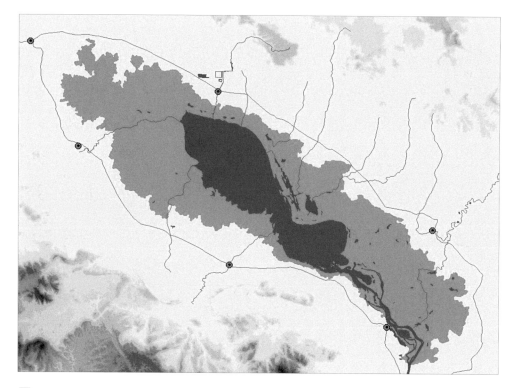

- ◼ dry season water level
- ◼ wet season water level

**Map of the Tonle Sap lake showing the Tonle Sap river to the bottom right, the numerous other smaller rivers that enter the lake and the water levels in the wet and dry season**

At the southernmost reaches of the Tonle Sap Lake the open water enters a maze of channels and backwaters where low water exposes extensive mudflats, providing a resource for thousands of migratory birds – and at one time even flamingos. This is the point where the lake ends and the Tonle Sap River – the tributary that connects the 'Great Lake' to the 'Mighty Mekong' – begins. It is one of the region's great untouched deltas, where there are no roads, bridges or dredged shipping lanes, and where ongoing accretion and erosion creates an environment that changes from year to year. It is the 'estuary' to the 'mangrove' of the Tonle Sap swamp forest, yet it is hundreds of kilometres from the sea.

For eight months the water in the Tonle Sap River flows south out of the lake, through the delta, downriver past Phnom Penh to join the Mekong. Then in June things all change. Snow melt in the uplands of Tibet, combined with wet season rain from the Annamite Mountains of Laos and Vietnam, causes the Mekong to rise. When the water level in the Mekong at Phnom Penh becomes higher than that in the lake, the Tonle Sap River reverses and the water starts to flow 'upriver', north past Phnom Penh and into the lake. This continues until late September, when the Mekong stops rising and the water level at Phnom Penh again becomes lower than that in the Tonle Sap Lake. At this point the Tonle Sap River turns again and flows back out of the lake.

Water continues flowing out of the Tonle Sap throughout the dry season and the lower the minimum water level in the Mekong at Phnom Penh, the lower the Tonle Sap Lake. It is also estimated that at this time

The delta of the Tonle Sap river
in wet season flood shortly
before it enters the lake,
Kompong Chhnang

A mixed flock of Great Egrets, Grey Herons and cormorants on the Tonle Sap lake shore, Battambang

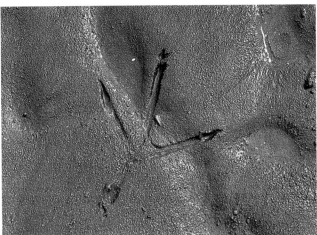

the lake contributes about 16% of the low season water in the Mekong downstream from Phnom Penh. Not only is the Tonle Sap an overflow valve, opening to divert excess water during the flood, but it is also a reservoir continuing to supply water through the dry season. The impacts of water levels in the Tonle Sap Lake throughout the year are felt all the way downstream to the delta[100].

Detailed records of water levels from the Mekong River exist since the early part of the century. On the Tonle Sap Lake a recording station at Kompong Luoung was operated daily from 1923 until 1965, and again from 1999 to the present day. Data from these stations give a good indication of just how important the water flow from the Mekong is to the level of the Tonle Sap. In an average year water from the Mekong is thought to contribute to around 60% of the total flood volume of the lake, 50% of this coming up the Tonle Sap River and 10% from overland flood between Kratie and Phnom Penh. The back flow from the Mekong along the Tonle Sap River is particularly important early in the flood season – June and July – before the Cambodian rains begin in earnest, while the contribution of the surrounding catchment is believed to be more significant later in the season[101]. However, as there has been no long-term monitoring on most local rivers that flow directly into the lake, further data is required to support this assumption.

It's not just water that enters the Tonle Sap during the wet season, as the rising flood carries with it the riches of the Mekong – large amounts of silt, critical to the productivity of the whole system.

A recurring fear, expressed regularly since the 1960s, has been that this sediment is rapidly filling up the lake, and the Tonle Sap will soon cease to exist. A 1990 report to the Mekong River Secretariat, stated "The lake appears to be in the final stage of ecological succession leading to its disappearance as an open water body. Considering the fact that the average depth of the lake in the dry season is now not more than 40cm, the time remaining for saving the lake is running out fast"[102]. For much of the 1990s this became the established way of thinking and such doomsday scenarios were often repeated, particularly in critiques of the Cambodian forestry sector[103, 104].

However by 1995 this theory was being independently questioned[105] and studies since the late 1990s using modern techniques of coring, radiocarbon analysis and hydrodynamic modelling, have provided new unequivocal data. Based on radiocarbon aging of sediments cores taken from the lake, it is now estimated that the sedimentation rate over the last 5,000 years has been approximately 0.1 mm/year. This equates to an accumulation on the lake bottom of only 50cm since the lake's formation and as little as 10cm since Angkorian times. Also rates have not increased in recent years. It is now understood that the danger of the lake filling up with sediment, even in the medium-term, is insignificant[106].

The Mekong, primarily via the Tonle Sap River, is responsible for by far the majority of sediment coming into the lake, with current estimates at more than 70% of the total[107]. Much of the sedimentation occurs immediately where the Tonle Sap River enters the open water of the lake. This creates a nutrient rich feeding ground for

**The still water of the wet season swamp forest, Prek Toal, Battambang**

resident and migratory waterbirds. At the turn of the century this mud loving bird community even included Greater Flamingos. However, with the last record from 1935 they are now extinct on the lake. The assumption is that this large bird, that lays its eggs on the ground in mud nests, would have been very susceptible to human persecution[108].

Although much of the sediment is deposited as soon as it enters the lake, what happens to the remainder? Travelling across the lake in the wet season, there is a noticeable change in the water colour. While in the centre the water is a milky coffee-like brown, in the swamp forest it is crystal clear. Conditions on the lake are strongly affected by the alternating monsoons, the southwest from May to October and northeast from November to April. Although winds are rarely very strong, they are sufficient to create significant wave-induced currents in the shallow, open water. These currents disturb and re-suspend sediment, mixing the water and making it turbid. On the contrary, in the swamp forest, the sheltering effect of the vegetation makes the water much calmer[109].

It is therefore in the still conditions of the vegetated floodplain that much of the silt is deposited, rather than in the permanent lake area where the continual movement prevents this from happening. The result is that within only a few hundred metres of the open lake the water of the swamp forest becomes so clear that when the sun reaches its highest point, underwater life is visible metres down. It is this clarity and light that allows the trees to continue to photosynthesise under water and for many fish to feast on the fruits of the swamp forest.

The amount of sediment entering the Tonle Sap every year strongly reflects annual variations in water levels. In a dry year the amount of Mekong silt reaching the lake is limited, while in a high flood year much larger amounts of sediment are widely dispersed around the floodplain. Over the years this process of depositing sediment not in, but around the lake, has contributed significantly to the fertility of the floodplain. Understanding this link is critically important, as it is this annual supply of both water and silt, that underpins the whole Tonle Sap ecosystem and with it the rice harvest, fish catch and ultimately millions of Cambodian lives.

As the water flows into the Tonle Sap during the flood it also carries with it, along with the sediment, millions of fish larvae. These are the 'white' migratory fish, and over the months of the wet season they will grow and

A stormy day on the open lake, Kbal Toal, Pursat

Submerged trees in the clear water of the wet season swamp forest, Prek Toal, Battambang

TOP:
**Sorting fish from the *dai* fishery, Prek Phneou, Kandal**

ABOVE:
**Transferring *trey riel* caught in the *dai* fishery, Prek Phneou, Kandal**

fatten on the inundated floodplain in preparation for the change in water direction and their return journey. This is the greatest natural phenomenon of Cambodia and will take them out of the lake and hundreds of kilometres on up the Mekong to breed as far away as southern Laos.

From late October until mid-March it is fishing season on the Tonle Sap River. The most important species, making up around 50% of the total river catch during these months, is the small cyprinid *trey riel*. This amazing fish, lives off microscopic algae and although short lived is prolific – each female breeds in the first year and produces thousands of eggs. Most remarkable, however, is not its productivity but the regularity of its annual migration, which always peaks en-masse in a short window of between one and six days before the first full moon of the year. The reasons are unknown, but it has happened, like clockwork, every January in living memory[110].

In anticipation of this annual migration a large local fishing industry has developed. Huge stationary nets, known as *dais*, are placed in rows across the river. In the same way as fishing lots on the lake, each *dai* is auctioned to the highest bidder who gains the right to operate the bag net for a set period. *Dais* have been used in this way since the late 19th century and there are currently fifteen rows along the river from Kompong Chhnang to Phnom Penh. Each has a large trawl like bag net staked in the water facing north towards the lake. The length of the net is over 100m, with an open mouth measuring about 25m wide by a few metres (the full depth of the river) deep. The mouth channels all migrating fish that enter into a bag at the end of the net. The bag is then hauled to the surface manually with ropes and pulleys and the fish unloaded into waiting boats. One bag can hold up to half a tonne of fish, and at the peak migration period, *dai* operators have to lift the bag every 15 to 20 minutes, throughout the day and night. If they leave the net in the water longer it is too heavy to lift, and the bag has to be opened and the catch released.

This is the best-known fishery in Cambodia, with catch data collected regularly from 1995. Over this period the total catch has ranged from 9,000 to 16,000 tonnes per year, equivalent to millions of dollars in local fish prices alone. This data set has also allowed fisheries biologists to examine the relationship between water levels in the Tonle Sap flood and the yield of migratory fish. They have discovered that for many of these species, particularly *trey riel*, lower water results in a lower fish catch[111, 112].

Unloading a full net of *trey riel*
on the *dai* fishery at dawn,
Prek Phneou, Kandal

Making *prahok* on the shore of the Tonle Sap River, Prek Phneou, Kandal

Piles of fish and *prahok* making
on the shore of the Tonle Sap
River, Prek Phneou, Kandal

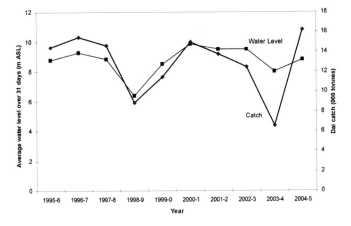

The speculation is that the sediment in the floodwater carries with it nutrients that are a critical part of the food chain and therefore the diet of these fish. Put simply, more water equals more sediment, equals more nutrients, equals more fish and ensures the livelihoods of millions of Cambodians.

However, the most recent data on catches of *trey riel* indicate that even this most resilient of fish maybe showing signs of pressure from over-exploitation. The total yields from the 2003 and 2004 *dai* fishing seasons have dropped below the levels expected from the flood versus fish relationship[112]. There could be multiple reasons for this, but one of them could just be the first signs of over-fishing.

*Trey riel* is critical to the Cambodian economy because it forms the basis of the national protein staple – *prahok* – a fermented fish paste upon which Cambodian rural families survive through the dry season. The annual Tonle Sap migration is not just of fish, but of people, when every January thousands of Cambodians travel the length of the country, traditionally by ox-cart, to barter part of their rice harvest for the next year's supply of *prahok*.

The process of making *prahok* takes place there and then on the bank of the river. The scales, heads and guts are removed and the fish thoroughly cleaned by treading in water. They are then soaked overnight, dried and salted before being stored in large ceramic pots to ferment. Nothing is wasted, the heads and guts are used for animal feed or fertiliser, and the fat for soap. The whole process creates a distinctive pungent aroma which can be smelt all the way downriver in the affluent expatriate riverside bars of Phnom Penh.

BELOW:
**Old man trading rice on the shore of the Tonle Sap River, Prek Phneou, Kandal**

RIGHT:
**People trading rice for *prahok* on the shore of the Tonle Sap River, Prek Phneou, Kandal**

BOTTOM:
**Bags of rice and piles of fish on the shore of the Tonle Sap River, Prek Phneou. Kandal**

**Traditional dancer on the bow of a racing boat, Phnom Penh**

For rural Cambodians this journey to Phnom Penh to sell rice marks the end of the rice harvest. However, many will have also travelled to the capital only two months earlier, to celebrate one of the Cambodia's biggest annual events, the water festival, or *om tuk* (boat racing) in Khmer. Although the origin of this festival is often linked to the turning of the Tonle Sap River, the water direction changes over a very narrow time period between mid-September and early October every year, a full four to six weeks before *om tuk*. Instead it is traditionally a festival that marks the beginning of the rice harvest.

As with many important events in the rural Cambodian year *om tuk*, is, like the migration of the *trey riel*, linked to the cycles of the lunar calendar. Held over the first full moon in November the festival celebrates the start of the harvest and gives thanks for the rice crop to come. Central to this is the preparation and eating of *ambok*, the first, as yet unripe, rice of the harvest, cooked in earthenware pots, pounded to remove the husk, then offered in prayer to the full moon. Today, for three days every year, the population of Phnom Penh swells as tens of thousands of people travel to the capital, sleeping on the streets, camping in makeshift shelters or living on boats, to take part in the festivities. The main event is the boat racing, where villagers, representing pagodas from across the country, compete on a course down the Tonle Sap River ending at the confluence with the Mekong in front of the Royal Palace and the King.

The tradition of royalty and boat racing goes back to Angkorian times and current-day boat racing may have its history in the 12th century and the great navy of Jayavarman VII. It is said that he presided over annual races both for training and to select boats for the battles. The reliefs of the Bayon depict Jayavarman VII leading his navy to liberate Angkor by defeating the Cham on the waters of the Mekong or Tonle Sap. Another theory is that the races have continued to this day in celebration of his glorious victory. By overseeing the event and presenting the prizes the present king maintains this link with the past.

The Royal Palace occupies a strategic and auspicious position overlooking Chaktamuk – the four directions – the Tonle Sap, the Mekong upstream and downstream and the Bassac. On the river side in front of the palace is a small shrine Preah Ang Dongkar which legend has is occupied by a very powerful spirit. Today it is a place where Cambodians go to give thanks when returning from a journey or overcoming hardship. As part of this many people make offerings by releasing small birds from cages, and a significant business has grown up trapping, trading and selling birds for release at Preah Ang Dongkar and other similar auspicious locations.

The primary birds involved in this trade are small agricultural birds, caught from rice fields outside Phnom

**Training for the boat races, Siem Reap**

FAR LEFT:
**Crowds watching the boat races along the Phnom Penh riverfront**

LEFT:
**Racing boats at Chaktamuk, the junction of the Tonle Sap, Mekong and Bassac Rivers**

same areas, where they feed in the same fields as ducks and chickens. Tests carried out in Thailand have shown these species can be potential carriers of the lethal H5N1 bird flu virus[115]. As well-meaning Cambodians hold these birds up to their face in prayer before release, the potential risk to their health is self-evident.

The Phnom Penh municipal authorities have made an excellent job of closing down wildlife sales which up until recent years occurred openly alongside domestic animals and birds in the city's markets. In the interest of both conservation and hygiene this was comparatively straight forward, but stopping a religious tradition, one which the king himself continues weekly, may be a lot more difficult, however dangerous it could be to peoples' health.

Those in control of Phnom Penh and its development face many challenges as the city's population grows. Its location, once of great strategic advantage, is now a major constraint to the functioning of a modern, urban economy. Phnom Penh was founded in the 15th century around the hill where Wat Phnom currently stands. By the end of the 19th century it was a growing port town of dykes and functioning canals. The city expanded over the centuries through the continued construction of concentric dykes followed by land-filling. Many of the major roads of modern Phnom Penh – Monivong, Sihanouk and Mao Tse Tung Boulevards – were all originally built upon dykes[116]. Throughout the city's early growth, canals and *boengs* (water bodies) were maintained as part of the natural drainage and flood management system.

As Phnom Penh has continued to expand, particularly in recent years, growth has been haphazard, and the

Penh. Among the most popular are resident munias and weavers and, in winter, migratory Yellow-breasted Buntings[113]. The birds are transported in cramped conditions and many arrive for sale sick and dying. Studies of munias caught for release in Indonesia indicate that they have an extremely high mortality rate and up to 50% may die within the first 24 hours of capture[114]. Several of these species are known to have declined, particularly over the past 50 years.

Of greater immediate concern is the risk that these small birds may potentially carry diseases such as avian influenza. Avian influenza – bird flu – has already been found in on poultry farms in Cambodia, including in areas close to Phnom Penh. Many of the sparrows, munias and weavers for sale on the waterfront come from the very

Releasing Baya Weavers at Preah Ang Dongkar, Phnom Penh

LEFT:
**Fireworks at the end of the *om tuk* festival, Phnom Penh**

RIGHT
**Phnom Penh and the Royal Palace at dusk from across the Tonle Sap River at Chroy Chongvar**

original drainage system has been compromised. In heavy rain, parts of the city regularly flood as drainage channels are now blocked, and pumps ineffective. In a severe flood year Phnom Penh remains vulnerable. A flood nearing 12 metres above sea-level could endanger the dykes[117] and overwhelm pumping capacity in the city centre. Despite this, potentially catastrophic development still continues inside and outside the city. The area around Prek Phneou, north of the Kop Srou dyke, one of the most important water holding areas on the edge of Phnom Penh, has over recent years been continually filled for industrial and agricultural development.

Floods, traditionally Cambodia's friend – an annual bounty upon which people relied – are now becoming an enemy that demands control. But an enemy to whom? Not to the rural Cambodians who still depend upon the water for their livelihoods, but to the urban wealthy who are slowly becoming detached from their rural roots.

LEFT:
**Modern day children of Phnom Penh enjoying the water of the new Phnom Penh Waterpark rather than the river**

BELOW:
**A family day out under the "waterfall" at the Phnom Penh Waterpark**

# PROTECTED ISLANDS: THE FLYING-FOXES OF KOH THOM

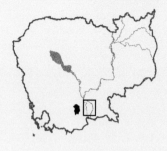

Koh Thom – an island in the Bassac river just outside of Phnom Penh – is famous for two things. Cambodians know it as one of the best fruit and vegetable growing areas close to the city, while followers of Buddhist meditation know it as the home of the Cambodian Vipassana Centre. Few know that the island's pagoda, Wat Kompong Kor, is also home to one of the most significant flying-fox (fruit bat) colonies left in the country.

These flying-foxes were once common wherever there was water, forming large roosts in the swamp forest of the Tonle Sap and along the Mekong, Tonle Sap and Bassac rivers. However, over the years they have been hunted in large numbers, both for local consumption and for sale to serve a thriving restaurant demand in Phnom Penh, so much so that they are now in danger of disappearing from Cambodia entirely. One of the largest bats in the world, flying-foxes are crucially important to local agriculture, as they are natural pollinators and seed dispersers of many commercially important fruit trees including banana, durian and mango.

To understand more about the conservation needs of these animals, a Cambodian biologist from the Ministry of Environment, An Dara, began a project with WCS to radio-track flying-foxes around Phnom Penh. He caught and placed transmitters on three bats from the roost at Wat Phnom. By regularly following them at night over a period of weeks he discovered that not only did they vary feeding sites each evening, but he tracked them flying up to 80km in a single night. They were ranging to feed over a potential area of thousands of square kilometres[118].

This has major implications for their conservation, as it means that protection cannot only be focussed at roosts and a few key local feeding sites, but will entail work across a wide area to raise awareness of the importance of the species. An excellent start has already been made with campaigns in schools and on national television, while government officials have enforced the law by seizing and releasing flying-foxes from Phnom Penh restaurants.

On the island of Koh Thom the flying-fox roost has long been protected. Here, not only have the monks provided security for the bats roosting within the pagoda, but they have also worked to persuade the local villagers not to kill the bats outside the pagoda. Perhaps as many as half of Cambodia's remaining regular flying-fox roosts are in the grounds of pagodas. And bats are not the only inhabitants as biologists are now coming across nesting and roosting sites of large waterbirds, such as herons and egrets, taking advantage of similar islands of protection provided by pagodas. The role of Buddhist temples, such as Wat Kompong Kor, as local nature reserves is one of increasing, but thus far little recognised, importance throughout Cambodia[119].

**The abbot and monks at the temple Wat Kompong Kor, Koh Thom, Kandal**

ABOVE LEFT:
**An Dara observing the flying-foxes with the monks at the temple Wat Kompong Kor, Koh Thom, Kandal**

ABOVE:
**One of the few major colonies of Grey Herons in the region is nesting inside the temple of Wat Prey Preuk Sa, Takeo**

LEFT:
**Roosting flying-foxes safe inside the temple of Wat Kompong Kor, Koh Thom, Kandal**

# THE CAMBODIAN MEKONG

The Khone Falls, Cambodia-Lao border

In June 1866 a French naval expedition left the maritime port of Saigon, destination China. They did not follow the traditional route through the South China Sea, but instead headed up the Mekong into Cambodia. The purpose of their journey was to navigate a passage to Yunnan and in doing so open a new gateway for the colonial authorities to access the rich heartland of southern China. Although the expedition was to eventually reach China, their quest, as that of several subsequent French explorers, was doomed to ultimate failure. One European pioneer after another, in search of fame and fortune, struggled through the rapids of northern Cambodia only to meet, at the Cambodia-Lao border, the impenetrable barrier of the Khone Falls[120].

Travelling upriver from the delta, these early explorers would have seen the Cambodian Mekong as it is today, a broad slow-flowing river, easily accessible in their steam-powered vessels. However, when they reached the town of Kratie everything changed, as just to the north, the village of Kompi marks the start of the Sambor rapids, and the Mekong becomes swift, rocky and dangerous. Eventually, the French authorities managed to blast and chart a route through these rapids, and the concrete channel markers they constructed, 600 of which are remarkably still in place[121], are used to this day by local river traffic travelling between Kratie and the northern town of Stung Treng.

The Khone Falls have still never been conquered for commercial river traffic. However, the colonial French did eventually come up with a bizarre and expensive navigable solution – laying a railway line, complete with locomotive,

Trees on the Mekong River
north of Stung Treng in the dry
season, the roots shaped by the
wet season force of the water

docks and cranes, on an island in the middle of the falls. Passengers or goods were disembarked above or below the falls and transported by rail to a craft awaiting them on the other side. While it never succeeded in opening up the river in the way they had hoped – it took 37 days and required at least seven changes of vessel to travel from Saigon to Luang Prabang, Laos[122] – the rail link operated for forty years, only coming to an end in 1940 when the Second World War reached Indochina.

Although a barrier to the mass movement of people, the Mekong rapids of northern Cambodian are a critical part of the migratory journey for large numbers of fish. A mosaic of sand and gravel islands, rocks and boulders, the river in these stretches alternates between shallow rapids and deep pools. Fifty-eight such pools have been documented in the stretch of river north from Kratie to the Khone Falls, some up to 80m deep[123]. These natural holes are the ultimate dry season destination of all the fish migrating out of the Tonle Sap as the water level drops.

Fish as diverse in size as the Mekong Giant Catfish and *trey riel* remain upriver, in the security of the deep water, throughout the dry months. With the onset of the rain and the rise again of the river they spawn and the flood carries their young larvae downstream onto the Tonle Sap floodplain and beyond. As such these pools are critical to the maintenance not only of local fish stocks, but of the whole Cambodian fishery system downstream to the delta of Vietnam.

The habitat mosaics of these rapids are important not only to migratory fish, but a whole range of resident species, many restricted only to these stretches. These include both unique Mekong fish and populations of endangered turtles, otters, dolphins and riverine birds. Historically these parts of the lower river supported colonies of fish-eating birds such as Indian Skimmer, River Tern and Black-bellied Tern. The first is extinct throughout the Mekong with no sightings since the early 1960s[124], and the last is now down to only two pairs breeding along the Sesan, a Mekong tributary in Ratanakiri Province[125]. All ground-nesting birds, their nests have always been vulnerable to collection by communities up and down the river. Without some form of protection a similar fate awaits the River Tern and other such birds confined to the river channel.

So far, it is only the remoteness of this area that has allowed these birds to survive. The length of the Mekong from Kratie to the Lao border has, in addition to the poor

river access, even worse road access, and up until the late 1990s was largely off-limits due to security concerns. There are comparatively few villages and minimal human disturbance. This has resulted in the preservation of an extensive area of natural habitat not found anywhere else in the basin. In recognition of the unique nature of this, the Mekong upstream from Stung Treng to the Lao border has been designated by the Cambodian government as a Wetland of International Importance under the Ramsar Convention on Wetlands. However, the river downstream to Kratie, which is probably even more important for conservation of both fish stocks and globally unique biodiversity, remains unprotected.

This remoteness has also meant that there are still discoveries to be made. The description of a bird species new to science is an unusual event, particularly in mainland Southeast Asia, yet in 2000 that's exactly what happened here. The Mekong Wagtail is a small, black and white bird that is now known to be endemic to the Mekong. It occurs only on rapid stretches of the river and tributaries between Kratie and southern Laos. Although highly visible, as few ornithologists had ever been able to visit these areas it had remained overlooked. In 2001 it was officially named *Motacilla samveasnae* in honour of Sam Veasna, a pioneering Cambodian Government conservation official who had tragically died from cerebral malaria only a year previously[126].

Another remarkable recent discovery may shed further light on the geological history of the river. In March 1999 freshwater jellyfish were found in pools just below the Khone Falls. Unfortunately the complex state

One of the original channel markers placed by the French colonial authorities in the Mekong River north of Stung Treng

of jellyfish taxonomy makes their identification and relationship to marine jellyfish populations in the region very problematic[127]. Nevertheless, there are many other, long known, faunal links between the Mekong and the sea. These include Irrawaddy Dolphin, West Coast Blackhead Sea Snake[128] and many fish species traditionally thought of as marine in origin such as two species of stingray, and several flatfish[129]. They may point to a time when sea levels were higher and there was a much closer connection between the now freshwater parts of the Mekong and the sea. However, many fish have always moved between the Mekong and the sea. Recent isotope studies have confirmed that one species of catfish *Pangasius krempfi* migrates all the way upriver from the South China Sea to spawn above the Khone Falls[130].

A French paper from 1916 also pointed to another, perhaps unique, marine link, describing a new species of seahorse based on two dried specimens said to have been collected from rapids in the Mekong of southern Laos[131]. This was an exceptional find, the only freshwater seahorse known in the world. However, dried seahorses have long been a common item in Chinese pharmacies, and ichthyologist Tyson Roberts has proposed that it is far more

likely these specimens – now known to be of a marine species widespread in the region – were brought to Lao towns by traders. There is certainly no further evidence that seahorses have ever occurred in the Mekong.

Perhaps the most bizarre marine animal claimed to exist in the Mekong involves the recent story of the Naga. Around the year 2000 a photograph began to appear widely in the region showing a huge fish being held by a group of soldiers. It was titled "Queen of Nagas seized by American Army at Mekhong River, Laos Military Base on June 27, 1973 with the length of 7.80 meters." The Naga, an underwater serpent of Hindu and Buddhist mythology, has long been associated with the Mekong, and local communities in Thailand, Laos and Cambodia still believe that it lives in caves under the river. The appearance of this photograph confirmed those beliefs for many. However, it soon proved to be a hoax and is in fact of an Oarfish *Regalecus glesne*, the world's longest fish, usually confined to the deep oceans. This particular animal was found by US soldiers on a beach near a military base in south California in 1996 – nowhere near the Mekong – and is now preserved at the Scripps Institute of Oceanography[132].

**Dry season sandbank in the
Mekong River near Sambor,
Kratie**

Dry season grassland at Boeng Prek Lapeou, Takeo, reflecting what much of the delta may once have looked like before conversion to rice

Downstream from Phnom Penh towards the sea, most of the Mekong's natural habitat has long gone. The Vietnamese delta, once known as the Plain of Reeds is now a plain of irrigated rice. A vast, monotonous, monoculture, with the only natural habitat confined to tiny, shrinking islands. The last significant remnant of the true delta is Boeng Prek Lapou, 10,000ha in southern Cambodia's Takeo Province. A seasonally inundated grassland forming vast mats of floating vegetation during the flood, it represents what Vietnam has long lost and what the whole delta would have once looked like.

Boeng Prek Lapou was only discovered by government biologists in 2000 due to the presence of Sarus Cranes. An emblem of the Mekong Delta, they were considered restricted to two small remaining areas in Vietnam. Boeng Prek Lapou was rapidly found to be the most important site for Sarus Cranes anywhere in the delta. Yet at the same time it was threatened by an agricultural development project that would convert the last remaining natural wetland into irrigated rice. Fortunately this was stopped and the area is now being proposed by the Government for protection as a Crane Conservation Area[133].

Uncoordinated development, particularly between countries sharing watersheds, is the greatest threat to the future of the Mekong ecosystem. The Sesan, Sekong and Srepok are the three great tributary rivers of north-east Cambodia. Rising in the mountains of Vietnam and Laos they come together to join the Mekong at Stung Treng. In 2001 the Vietnamese began operation of the Yali Falls dam on the Sesan – the first of a cascade of four such

TOP AND ABOVE:
**Sarus Cranes, Boeng Prek Lapeou, Takeo**

hydro-power projects they plan for the river. Although only 70km upstream of the Cambodian border, the Cambodians were never consulted on its construction.

For the purposes of the original Yali Falls EIA – conducted with Swiss Government funding for the Mekong River Commission (MRC) – the downstream area was defined as only 8km below the dam, thus ignoring Cambodia totally. In addition, after completion of the dam, the Vietnamese authorities gave the Cambodians no prior warnings of water releases, resulting in deaths of local people living along the river and an international incident.

Local villagers have also reported negative impacts on the Sesan's fisheries, and increased siltation has apparently decreased the depth of one of the river's most important deep pools from 7-8m to just half a metre[134]. In 2003 a study on the Sesan's breeding birds demonstrated the impacts of changing flow regimes on some of the region's most at-risk bird populations. Not only were changing patterns of sedimentation and erosion reducing available habitat, but 50% of River Lapwing nests located during the study were destroyed by sudden fluctuations in water released from the dam[135].

The most extreme example of the lack of consultation and cooperation over managing the shared water of the Mekong involves the upstream actions of China. China already has two hydropower dams – the Manwan and Dachaoshan – operating on the mainstream Mekong, another is well advanced and construction on a fourth has commenced. The third – the Xiaowan – will be the second largest in China after the Three Gorges. It is scheduled to be completed and filled by 2013, with a reservoir stretching 169km in length. Eventual plans for the Chinese Mekong are for a cascade of eight dams[136]. All are planned without any consultation with the downstream nations: Myanmar, Laos, Thailand, Cambodia and Vietnam.

The downstream impact of these projects is not fully understood, but they will undoubtedly significantly alter both the water and sediment flow patterns of the river. When the Manwan dam was first closed and began filling in 1993 the effect on water-levels was noticed downstream in both Thailand and Laos. It is claimed by some that when the dam cascade is finished the resulting increased dry season and decreased wet season flow will positively benefit those downstream, by lessoning the risk of both drought and flood.

Fishing amongst the flooded grass as the flood recedes, close to the Vietnamese border, Boeng Prek Lapeou, Takeo

Arguments for positive downstream benefits from dams on the Mekong, demonstrate a lack of understanding of the lower river's ecological systems and the lives of the people that depend on them. To rural communities in Cambodia floods are not a threat, but a source of wealth, upon which their rice-farming and fishing lifestyles have relied over centuries. Any significant decrease in wet season flow and a reduction in flood heights will put at risk the livelihoods of millions of people.

The dry season water level of 2004 was among the lowest on record in the lower Mekong, and created heated debate on the issues of shared water management. Some environmentalists blamed such low water levels on the upstream impacts of the Chinese dams, but this was disputed by the MRC who attributed the situation to unusually poor rainfall[137]. The official position of the Chinese government on such issues is that as the Mekong in China contributes only an estimated 16% of the river's total water flow, the downstream effects of any dam will be negligible. This view is apparently shared by the MRC, and echoed in an interview by the organisation's CEO in November 2004, while simultaneously perpetuating the myth that reduced floods would benefit communities downstream[138].

A major problem is that the basin-wide data on which the hydrological models for the Mekong are based – particularly that from upstream – is still too poor for any confident predictions. And the reality is, as an MRC official admitted in a 2004 interview with the *New Scientist* magazine, "the Chinese dams are so large, they are changing everything"[139]. Even if these dams did not, as

some are led to believe, significantly affect water regimes, what of the sediment flows? Data suggest that – partly due to the much higher gradients in the upper Mekong – China contributes an estimated 50% of the estimated 150-170 million tons/year of sediment load in the Mekong River[140]. The Manwan dam is already allegedly facing a shortened life due to rapid sedimentation, and the affects of decreased silt reaching the Tonle Sap floodplain could be just as severe on the fisheries as decreased water.

Whatever the downstream concerns, regional governments appear unable, or unwilling to challenge the Chinese. For poorer countries such as Laos or Cambodia, the Chinese are far too important a regional economic force and bilateral donor to risk taking to task. In addition, there seems to be no regional mechanism within which to discuss the issues. The MRC was formed in 1995, by the signing of the 'Agreement for the Sustainable Development of the Mekong River Basin' by Thailand, Laos, Cambodia and Vietnam, and part of its stated mission is "to promote and co-ordinate sustainable management and development of water and related resources for the countries' mutual benefit". China however, has always refused to become a member and in addition, the mandate of the MRC rests not with the institution but with the member governments. As a result it is completely toothless to effectively tackle any of these issues.

In the early 1990s the Asian Development Bank (ADB) formulated its Greater Mekong Subregion project, a loose forum of Mekong basin member governments, focused on regional development. It, too, has no regulatory authority, and although not directly funding any of the Chinese dams, it has a record of promoting such schemes. As recently as 2003, a report commissioned by the ADB recommended a regional power grid which would be based on a network of hydro-power generating dams across the Mekong basin.

Perhaps the only legal instrument available to the lower Mekong countries such as Cambodia is the provisions of the 1997 'Convention on the Law of the Non-navigational Use of International Watercourses' of the United Nations International Law Commission. This requires "an upstream country not to act in an inequitable fashion in relation to its use of rivers, so far as countries downstream are concerned"[141]. However, it appears that everyone in the Mekong Basin is happy to ignore this.

Worse, it seems that for some amongst the downstream governments an attitude of "if you can't beat them, join them…" prevails. There are currently significant Mekong tributary dams operational or planned in Laos, Thailand and Vietnam. Plans for mainstream dams on the lower Mekong come and go, but furthest downstream would be a dam across the Cambodian Mekong at Sambor, the very rapids that first prevented early navigation of the river. This was first proposed by Australian consultant engineers in the 1960s and would flood around 750 km². Although officially off the agenda, the project regularly rears its head again every few years.

Meanwhile, more than a century on, the grand plans of the French to make the Mekong a trade highway into China have been taken on again, this time by the Chinese themselves. In 2000, China signed an agreement on commercial navigation with Myanmar, Laos and Thailand to permit ships of up to 500 tonnes to trade between Yunnan and Luang Prabang, a distance of 886 kilometres. The maximum size of vessels previously able to navigate this stretch of the river was only 120 tonnes, so to allow larger ships to pass, China agreed to carry out the removal of all major rapids, shoals and reefs that obstructed navigation. As with the dam developments, downstream countries – Cambodia and Vietnam – were not consulted.

According to Tyson Roberts the eventual Chinese goal is actually to succeed where the French failed, and make the Mekong navigable all the way to the South China Sea[142]. The construction of the upstream dams is also a tool to that end, allowing the maintenance of navigable water levels throughout the dry season. This has already occurred, as during the very low-water levels of March-April 2004 extra water was released from the Manwan and Dachaoshan dams to raise the river level and enable cargo to continue to trade between Yunnan and Chiang Saen, Thailand[143].

On 1st May 2004, after three years of clearing, the first 300-tonne Chinese vessel reached Chiang Saen[144]. In 2004 more than 3,000 vessels are expected to dock at Chiang Saen, up from less than 1,000 in 2003, and plans are underway to build a second port capable of handling ships of 500 tonnes[145]. However, plans to proceed down river to Luang Prabang are now on hold following concerns from the Thai government over the effect of the blasting on the position of its border with Laos, and mounting protests from Thai NGOs, who not only effectively critiqued the original flawed EIA, but also illustrated

ABOVE:
**The upper Mekong River below the sacred Mount Kartabo near Deqin, Yunnan, China**

LEFT:
**The Manwan Dam on the upper Mekong River, southern Yunnan, China**

the negative effects of the ongoing development on local river-dependent communities.

Encouragingly the active involvement of academics and NGOs in these controversies, not just in Southeast Asia but also in China, is bringing about an increased understanding of the importance of regional water management issues. They are both raising awareness, and perhaps more importantly, bringing much needed data to inform the debate. In 2004 senior levels of the Chinese government suspended plans for a series of dams on the Salween River, a sister river of the Mekong flowing into Myanmar, citing concerns voiced by Chinese scientists and environmentalists[146]. While more recently the chief engineer of the Yangtze River Water Resources Commission warned that further exploitation of the Yangtze's upper reaches for hydro-power would mean inevitable damage to the river's ecosystem[147]. Such changes in policy or comments from government officials would have been unthinkable even a few years ago.

Some in the region, searching for alternatives, are looking more closely at what is behind the ever-increasing power demands. What they have found is energy being wasted on a huge scale in both the public and private sectors. They propose for policies for more effective energy conservation and demand-side power management would significantly decrease the need for these large expensive showpiece development schemes[148]. Others have found more innovative and local solutions.

In Stung Treng Province, northern Cambodia, to supply power to his army camp and a nearby village a local soldier has built his own micro-generator on a small stream. He reportedly had never even seen a picture of a hydro-power station and designed his system solely using locally available materials, starting with an old ox-cart wheel[149].

Such positive initiatives, at whatever scale, must be encouraged, as without progress, issues of water management in the Mekong will inevitably escalate. The potential for disruption of crucial flood dependent ecosystems is so great that it warrants immediate attention. Significant changes in the annual flood regime could result not only in a complete failure of the Tonle Sap – Cambodia's heart – but also of floodplain systems in Laos, Thailand and Vietnam. The resulting impacts on fisheries, agriculture and therefore livelihoods throughout the lower basin could be catastrophic. Millions of starving and potentially displaced people would suddenly make this not just a regional concern for China and Southeast Asia, but an issue of international security.

The calmer waters of the Mekong River below the last rapids at Kompi, a little north of Kratie town

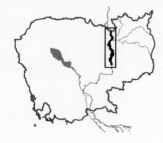

The story of how the dolphin came to be has been told to every Cambodian child for generations. Due to the greed of her parents, a young girl was married to a snake in the mistaken belief he was a god. On her wedding night she was eaten by the snake, but then rescued and cut out of his belly. Ashamed and to clean herself of the slime from the snake she dived into the river. She was never to return and became the first dolphin of the Mekong. To this day Cambodians believe dolphins are people and Khmer fishing communities along the Mekong will not kill them as it brings bad luck.

The Irrawaddy Dolphin is not uncommon in coastal areas from Southeast Asia to Australia, but true freshwater populations exist in only three rivers: the Mahakam in Indonesia, the Irrawaddy in Myanmar and the Mekong in Cambodia and Laos. In all they are under severe threat and populations are small and declining. Current research also indicates that these populations may well be genetically quite distinct and therefore perhaps of even greater conservation importance.

In 2001 Isabel Beasley, a PhD student from James Cook University, Australia, began working with counterparts from the Department of Fisheries on a research project examining the ecology and status of these special animals in the Mekong. The results have been frightening. There are now thought to be only around 100 dolphins left in the whole river, all confined to four key deep pool

areas of the Cambodian Mekong between Kratie and the Lao border. Current mortality rates of more than 10% every year suggest the population will soon be extinct unless urgent conservation measures are taken[150].

The primary threat is from incidental by-catch in large nylon mono-filament gill-nets. Fishermen place the nets, often for several days at a time, in deep pools targeting large valuable fish. Unfortunately these are the same areas favoured by the dolphins whose sonar cannot detect the fine artificial filaments, and they risk becoming entangled. After a short while trapped in such a net, an air-breathing dolphin drowns. In addition there is now concern that toxic chemicals used in gold mining on some of the Mekong tributaries may also be resulting in dolphin deaths, particularly of young animals.

In light of this knowledge, and imminent threats to the survival of the animals, Isabel and her Cambodian colleagues initiated a dolphin conservation project working with the Department of Fisheries, and in collaboration with WCS. Influential donor support including the British Embassy and the MRC was obtained and with this assistance a series of actions have been begun to secure the future of the dolphins. These include: increasing awareness of the plight of the dolphin amongst river communities, enforcing fishery laws and promoting a series of alternative income-generating schemes to relieve heavy fishing pressure in key dolphin areas. If successful, these initiatives would not only conserve dolphins, but the key fish-breeding stocks of the deep pools.

One of the activities central to the project is the promotion of managed dolphin watching ecotourism. Significant numbers of foreign tourists now visit two of the key areas to see dolphins, and if the income generated can be effectively managed to benefit the local fishermen and communities this represents a potential win-win solution. If the project is successful, not only foreigners, but future generations of Cambodians will still be able to see Irrawaddy Dolphins in the Mekong rather than only hearing about them in folk stories as children.

**Irrawaddy Dolphin drowned having been accidentally caught in a gill net between Kratie and Stung Treng**
**©Isabel Beasley**

ABOVE LEFT:
**A rare photograph of a young Irrawaddy Dolphin calf and its parent on the Cambodia-Lao border**
©Isabel Beasley

ABOVE:
**159TR Dolphin watching tourists, Kompi, Kratie**

LEFT:
**An Irrawaddy Dolphin that strayed to Kandal in the wet season of early 2002**
©Pete Davidson

# FOOTNOTES

[1] Global Witness (2001) *The credibility gap – and the need to bridge it.* p. 38. Global Witness (2002) *Deforestation without limits.* p. 19.

[2] Yi Thon (2002) The role of Buddhist wats and NGOs in environmental preservation in Cambodia. In Menon, V. and Sakamoto, M. (eds.) *Heaven and Earth and I: Ethics of Nature Conservation in Asia.* Penguin Books. New Delhi, India.

[3] Evans, T.D., Hout Piseth, Phet Phaktra and Hang Mary (2003) *A study of resin-tapping and livelihoods in southern Mondulkiri, Cambodia, with implications for conservation and forest management.* WCS Cambodia Program. Phnom Penh.

[4] Kiernan, B. (1996) *The Pol Pot Regime.* Yale University Press.

[5] Vong Sokheng and Cochrane, L. (2005) Rich and powerful snatching up land illegally in Siem Reap area. *Phnom Penh Post,* 14/08, April 22 - May 5, 2005.

[6] Roberts, T. (2003) Fish scenes and symbolism and kingship in the bas-reliefs of Angkor Wat and the Bayon. *Natural History Bulletin of the Siam Society* 50(2): 135-193.

[7] Poole, C.M. and Duckworth, J.W. (in press) A documented 20th century record of Javan Rhinoceros *Rhinoceros sondaicus* from Cambodia. *Mammalia.*

[8] Roberts, T. (2003) as 6 above.

[9] Rainboth, W.J. (1996) Fishes of the Cambodian Mekong. FAO, Rome.

[10] Engelbach, P. (1953) Les oiseaux d'Angkor et leur identification sur le terrain. *Terre et Vie* 100: 148-166.

[11] Goes, F. (2000) Vanishing birds of Angkor. *Cambodia Bird News* 5: 3-10.

[12] Jackson, B. (2001) *Kingfisher Blue.* Ten Speed Press. Berkeley.

[13] Miura, K. (2000) Social anthropological research on "The people of Angkor. Living within a World Heritage site". *Siksacakr* 2: 15-19.

[14] Kummu, M. (2003) *The natural environment and historical water management of Angkor, Cambodia.* Paper presented at the World Archaeological Congress, Washington D.C. June 2003.

[15] Roberts, T. (2003) as 6 above.

[16] Sanday, J. (1997) The triumphs and perils of Khmer architecture. In Jessup, H.I and Zéphir, T. *Sculpture of Angkor and ancient Cambodia: Millennium of glory.*

[17] Fletcher, R. (2003) Redefining Angkor: Structure and environment of the largest low density urban complex of the pre-industrial world. *Udaya* 4: 107-125.

[18] Vann Molyvann (2003) *Modern Khmer Cities.* Reyum. Phnom Penh.

[19] Wharton, C. H. (1957) *An ecological study of the Kouprey,* Novibos sauveli *(Urbain).* Manilla: Institute of Science and Technology.

[20] Higham, C. (2003) *The civilization of Angkor.* Phoenix, London.

[21] Helmers, K. (1996) Rice in the Cambodian economy: past and present pp. 1-25 in Nesbitt, H.J. (ed). *Rice production in Cambodia.* University Press. Phnom Penh.

[22] Ministry of Agriculture, Forestry and Fisheries. (2004) *Annual conference on agriculture, forestry and fisheries* (05-06 April 2004). Ministry of Agriculture, Forestry and Fisheries. Phnom Penh.

[23] Javier, E.L. (1996) Rice ecosystems and varieties pp. 72-133 in Nesbitt, H.J. (ed.) *Rice production in Cambodia.* University Press. Phnom Penh.

[24] Catling, D. (1992) *Rice in deep water.* IRRI and Macmillan Press. London.

[25] Catling, D (2001) *An overview of deepwater rice in Cambodia.* Unpublished report to UNDP Cambodia. Phnom Penh.

[26] Catling, D. (1992) as 24 above.

[27] Javier, E.L. (1996) as 23 above.

[28] Balzer, T., Balzer, P. and Pon, S. (2002) *Traditional use and availability of aquatic biodiversity in rice-based ecosystems. I. Kampong Thom Province, Kingdom of Cambodia.* FAO Inland Water Resources and Aquaculture Service. Rome.

[29] Gregory, R. (1997) *Ricefield Fisheries Handbook.* Cambodia-IRRI-Australia Project. Phnom Penh.

[30] Gregory, R. (1997) as 29 above.

[31] EJF. (2002) *Death in Small Doses: Cambodia's Pesticides Problems and Solutions.* Environmental Justice Foundation, London, UK.

[32] Nesbitt, H. J., Hickey, A. and Phirun, I. (1996) Adulterated pesticides in Cambodia. *International Rice Res. Notes* 21 (1): 51.

[33] In Monirith, Nakata, H., Tanabe, S. and Touch Seang Tana (1999) Persistent organochlorine residues in marine and freshwater fish in Cambodia. *Marine Pollution Bulletin* 38: 604-612.

[34] EJF. (2002) as 31 above.

[35] http://www.communityipm.org/ Countries/cambodia.htm

[36] Gregory, R. (1997) as 29 above

[37] Round P. (2002) A bright-green, poisoned landscape. *Bird Conservation Society of Thailand Bull.* 19 (5): 13-16.

[38] Roveda, V. (2003) The Ramayana and Khmer beliefs. *Udaya* 4: 53-57.

[39] Gum, W. (1998) *Natural resource management in the Tonle Sap Biosphere Reserve in Battambang Province.* Consultancy report to the European Commission Support Programme to the Environmental Sector in Cambodia. Phnom Penh.

[40] Keskinen, M. (2003) The Great Diversity of Livelihoods? – *Socioeconomic survey of the Tonle Sap Lake.* WUP-FIN Socio-economic Studies on Tonle Sap 8, MRCS/WUP-FIN, Phnom Penh.

[41] Degen, P and Nao Thuok (1998) *Inland Fishery Management in Cambodia: Is the concept of community-based management appropriate for fishing lots?* Paper presented at the Seventh Conference of the International Association for the Study of Common Property, Vancouver Canada, 10-14 June 1998.

[42] Van Zalinge, N., Nao Thuok and Sam Nuov (2001) Status of the Cambodian Inland Capture Fisheries with Special Reference to the Tonle Sap Great Lake. In *Cambodia Fisheries Technical Paper Series, Volume III,* Inland Fisheries Research and Development Institute of Cambodia (IFReDI), Phnom Penh.

[43] Keskinen, M. (2003) as 40 above.

[44] Gum, W. (1998) as 39 above.

[45] Platt, S.G., Heng S., Long K., Stuart, B.L. and Thorbjarnarson, J.B. (in press) Population status and conservation of wild Siamese Crocodiles *(Crocodylus siamensis)* in the Tonle Sap Biosphere Reserve, Cambodia. *Natural History Bulletin of the Siam Society.*

[46] Thorbjarnarson, J., Heng Sovannara and Long Kheng (2004) *Siamese Crocodile Farming* and *Conservation in Cambodia. A Review with Recommendations.* Paper Presented at the IUCN Crocodile Specialist Group Meeting, Darwin, Australia. May 2004.

[47] Daltry, J. et al. (2004) *Cambodia Country Summary: Siamese Crocodile Crocodylus siamensis.* Paper Presented at the IUCN Crocodile Specialist Group Meeting, Darwin, Australia. May 2004.

[48] Thorbjarnarson, J., Heng Sovannara and Long Kheng (2004) as 46 above.

[49] Thorbjarnarson, J., Heng Sovannara and Long Kheng (2004) as 46 above.

[50] Platt, S.G., Heng S., Long K., Stuart, B.L. and Thorbjarnarson, J.B. (in press) as 45 above.

[51] Thorbjarnarson, J., Heng Sovannara and Long Kheng (2004) as 46 above.

[52] Platt, S.G., Holloway, R.H.P., Evans, P.T., Kiran Paudyal, Has Piron, and Rainwater, T. R. (in press) Physical evidence for the historic occurrence of Estuarine Crocodiles *(Crocodylus porosus* Schneider, 1801) in Tonle Sap, Cambodia. *Hamadryad.*

[53] Holloway, R.H.P. (2003) Domestic trade of tortoises and freshwater turtles in Cambodia. *Chelonian Conservation Biology* 4(3): 733-734.

[54] Jahn, G.C., Kiev, B., Pheng, S. and Pol, C. (1996). Pest management in rice. pp. 134-147 in Nesbitt, H.J. (ed). *Rice production in Cambodia.* University Press. Phnom Penh.

[55] Carlsson, N.O.L, Brönmark, C. and Hansson, L. (2004) Invading herbivory: the Golden Apple Snail alters ecosystem functioning in Asian wetlands. *Ecology* 85(6): 1575–1580.

[56] Round P. (2002) as 37 above.

[57] Welcomme, R. and Chavalit Vidthayanom. (2003) *The impacts of introductions and stocking of exotic species in the Mekong Basin and policies for their control.* MRC Technical Paper No. 9, Mekong River Commission, Phnom Penh.

[58] Campbell, I.C., Poole, C.M. Giesen, W. and Valbo-Jorgensen, J. (in press) Comparative biodiversity value of large wetlands: Tonle Sap Great Lake, Cambodia. *Aquatic Sciences.*

[59] Welcomme, R. and Chavalit Vidthayanom. (2003) as 57 above.

[60] Campbell, I.C., Poole, C.M. Giesen, W. and Valbo-Jorgensen, J. (in press) as 58 above.

[61] *Mimosa pigra* L.Weed Info Sheet 11. (1992) The Southeast Asian Weed Information Centre (SEAWIC). Bogor, Indonesia.

[62] Campbell, I.C., Poole, C.M. Giesen, W. and Valbo-Jorgensen, J. (in press) as 58 above.

[63] Triet T, Thi NL, Storrs MJ, Kiet LC. (2001) The value of awareness and early intervention in the management of alien invasive species: a case-study on the eradication of *Mimosa pigra* at the Tram Chim National Park. In *Assessment and management of alien species that threaten ecosystems, habitats and species:* abstracts of keynote addresses and posters presented at the sixth meeting of the Subsidiary Body on Scientific, Technical and Technological Advice. CBD Technical Series no. 1. Montreal: Secretariat of the Convention on Biological Diversity. p 37-8.

[64] Triet T, Thi NL, Storrs MJ, Kiet LC. (2001) as 63 above.

[65] Sugita, R. and Goto, A. (2004) Chong Kneas Environmental Improvement Project. *Tonle Sap Watch Newsletter.* 1: 4-5.

[66] Middleton, C.,Vann Piseth and Pen Raingsey (eds.) (2004) News in Brief. *Tonle Sap Watch Newsletter.* 2: 2.

[67] Middleton, C.,Vann Piseth and Pen Raingsey (eds.) (2004) as 66 above.

[68] Middleton, C. and Mak Sithirith (2004) An introduction to the ADB and its role in Tonle Sap Lake. *Tonle Sap Watch Newsletter.* 1: 2-3

[69] Daltry, J. et al. (2004) as 47 above.

[70] Mouhot, H. (2000) *Travels in Siam, Cambodia, Laos, and Annam.* Bangkok: White Lotus. Reprint.

[71] Van Zalinge, N. (2002) Update on the status of the Cambodian inland capture fisheries sector with special reference to the Tonle Sap Great Lake. *Catch and Culture* 8(2): 1-9.

[72] *United Nations Development Programme Cambodia Annual Report* 2003.

[73] Van Zalinge, N., Sam Nuov, Choulamany, X., Degen, P., Pongsri, C., Jensen, J. and Nguyen Van Hao (2003). *The Mekong River System.* Paper presented at the Second International Symposium on the Management of Large Rivers for Fisheries, Phnom Penh, 11-14 February 2003.

[74] Van Zalinge, N., Sam Nuov, Choulamany, X., Degen, P., Pongsri, C., Jensen, J. and Nguyen Van Hao (2003) as 73 above.

[75] Van Zalinge, N. (2002) as 71 above.

[76] Van Zalinge, N., Sam Nuov, Choulamany, X., Degen, P., Pongsri, C., Jensen, J. and Nguyen Van Hao (2003) as 73 above.

[77] Degen P., van Acker, F.,Van Zalinge, N.P., Nao Thuok and Deap Loeung. (2000) *Taken for granted. Conflicts over Cambodia's freshwater fish resources.* Paper presented at the IASCP Common Property Conference, Indiana, USA, 31 May - 4 June 2000.

[78] Fisheries Action Coalition Team (2001) *Feast or famine? Solutions to Cambodia's fisheries conflicts.* Environmental Justice Foundation, Phnom Penh.

[79] Fisheries Action Coalition Team (2001) as 78 above.

[80] Fisheries Action Coalition Team (2001) as 78 above.

[81] Stuart, B. L., Smith, J., Davey, K., Prom Din, and Platt. S. G. (2000) Homalopsine watersnakes: The harvest and trade from Tonle Sap. *TRAFFIC Bulletin* 18(3): 115-124.

[82] Van Zalinge, N. (2002) as 71 above.

[83] Van Zalinge, N., Sam Nuov, Choulamany, X., Degen, P., Pongsri, C., Jensen, J. and Nguyen Van Hao (2003) as 73 above.

[84] Van Zalinge, N. (2002) as 71 above.

[85] Van Zalinge, N., Sam Nuov, Choulamany, X., Degen, P., Pongsri, C., Jensen, J. and Nguyen Van Hao (2003) as 73 above.

[86] Hortle, K.G., Ngor Pengbun, Hem Rady and Lieng Sopha (2004) Trends in the Cambodian *dai* fishery: floods and fishing pressure. *Catch and Culture* 10(1): 7-9.

[87] Van Zalinge, N., Lieng Sopha, Ngor Peng Bun, Heng Kong, and Valbo Jørgensen, J. (2002) *Status of the Mekong* Pangasianodon hypophthal-mus *resources, with special reference to the stock shared between Cambodia and Viet Nam.* MRC Technical Paper No. 1, Mekong River Commission, Phnom Penh.

[88] Scroggins, H., (1998) Lucrative Trade in Baby Fish a Deadly Business. *Phnom Penh Post* 417 September 1998.

[89] Degen, P and Nao Thuok (1998) as 41 above.

[90] Hogan, Z.S., Moyle, P.B., May, B., Vander Zanden, M.J. and Baird, I.G. (2004) The Imperiled Giants of the Mekong - Ecologists struggle to understand - and protect – Southeast Asia's large migratory catfish. *American Scientist* 92 (3).

[91] Mouhot, H. (2000) as 70 above.

[92] Woodsworth, G. (1995) Disappearing Lakes - What is to be Done? A Case of the Tonle Sap, Cambodia. In *Proceedings of the Regional Dialogue on Biodiversity and Natural Resources Management in Mainland Southeast Asian Economies, Kunming, China, 21-24 February 1995.* Natural Resources and Environment Program of the Thailand Development Research Institute, and Kunming Institute of Botany (Chinese Academy of Sciences): 99-109.

[93] McDonald, A., Pech, B, Phauk,V. and Leeu, B. (1997) *Plant communities of the Tonle Sap Floodplain.* UNESCO, IUCN,Wetlands International and SPEC (European Commission), Phnom Penh.

[94] Gum,W. (1998) as 39 above.

[95] Mundkur,T., Carr, P., Sun, H. and Chhim, S. (1995) *Surveys for large waterbirds in Cambodia. March - April 1994.* IUCN/SSC. Cambridge, UK.

[96] Parr, J.W. K., Eames, J. C., Sun H., Hong C., Som H., Pich,V.L. and Seng, K.H. (1996) *Biological and social aspects of waterbird exploitation and natural resource utilization of Prek Toal,Tonle Sap Lake, Cambodia.* IUCN/SSC/ Cambridge, UK.

[97] Ear-Dupuy, H., Briggs, E., Hong C. and Keo, O. (1998) *Waterbird Conservation in the Prek Toal Area, Battambang Province, Cambodia.* Wetlands International, International Crane Foundation and the Wildlife Protection Office. Phnom Penh.

[98] Platt, S. G., Stuart, B. L., Heng Sovannara, Long Kheng, Kalyar, and Heng Kimchay. (2003). Rediscovery of the critically endangered river terrapin, Batagur baska, in Cambodia, with notes on occurrence, reproduction, and conservation status. *Chelonian Conservation and Biology* 4(3):691-695.

[99] Roberts, T. (2003) as 6 above.

[100] Campbell, I.C., Poole, C.M. Giesen, W. and Valbo-Jorgensen, J. (in press) as 58 above.

[101] Campbell, I.C., Poole, C.M. Giesen, W. and Valbo-Jorgensen, J. (in press) as 58 above.

[102] Csavas, I., (1990) *Report of the Mekong Secretariat Mission to Cambodia.* Mekong Secretariat, Bangkok.

[103] Global Witness (1995) *Forests, Famine and War- the Key to Cambodia's Future.*

[104] Global Witness (1996) *Corruption, War and Forest Policy – the Unsustainable exploitation of Cambodia's Forests.*

[105] Woodsworth, G. (1995) as 92 above.

106 Campbell, I.C., Poole, C.M. Giesen, W. and Valbo-Jorgensen, J. (in press) as 58 above.

107 Sarkkula J. and Koponen J. (2003) *Modelling Tonle Sap for Environmental Impact Assessment and Management Support*. Finnish Environment Institute.

108 Thomas, W.W. and Poole, C. M. (2003) An annotated list of the birds of Cambodia from 1859 to 1970. *Forktail*. 19: 103-127.

109 Sarkkula J. and Koponen J. (2003) as 107 above.

110 Van Zalinge, N., Deap Loeung, Ngor Pengbun, Sarkkula, J. and Koponen, J. (2003) *Mekong flood levels and Tonle Sap fish catches*. Paper presented at the Second International Symposium on the Management of Large Rivers for Fisheries, Phnom Penh, 11-14 February 2003.

111 Van Zalinge, N., Deap Loeung, Ngor Pengbun, Sarkkula, J. and Koponen, J. (2003) as 110 above.

112 Hortle, K.G., Ngor Pengbun, Hem Rady and Lieng Sopha (2005) Tonle Sap yields record haul. *Catch and Culture* 11(1): 3-7.

113 Van Zalinge, N. (1999) Sunday bird sales at Tonle Sap riverside. *Cambodia Bird News* 2: 30-33.

114 Shepherd, C. R., Sukumaran, J. and Wich, S. A . (2005) *The Live Wild Animal Pet Trade of Medan: Large and Largely Illegal – An analysis of the pet trade in Medan, Sumatra, 1997 – 2001*.TRAFFIC Southeast Asia.

115 Poole, C.M. and Gilbert, M. (2005) Do wild birds play any role in HPAI epidemics? *FAO AIDE News*. 10: 7-8.

116 Vann Molyvann (2003) as 18 above.

117 Vann Molyvann (2003) as 18 above.

118 An Dara (2002) *The Flying-foxes of Cambodia*. WCS Cambodia Program. Phnom Penh.

119 Yi Thon (2002) as 2 above.

120 Garnier F. (1996) *Travels in Cambodia and part of Laos. The Mekong Exploration Commission Report (1866-1868) – Volume 1*. White Lotus, Bangkok. Reprint.

121 Starr, P. (2003) *The People's Highway: Past, Present and Future Transport on the Mekong River System*. Mekong Development Series No. 3. Mekong River Commission, Phnom Penh.

122 Starr, P. (2003) as 121 above.

123 Poulsen, A, Ouch Poeu, Sintavong Viravong, Ubolratana Suntornratana and Nguyen Thanh Tung (2002) *Deep pools as dry season fish habitats in the Mekong Basin*. MRC Technical Paper No. 4, Mekong River Commission, Phnom Penh.

124 Thomas, W.W. and Poole, C. M. (2003) as 108 above.

125 Poole, C.M. (2003). Black-bellied Tern - the rarest bird in Cambodia? *Cambodia Bird News* 11: 26-31.

126 Duckworth, J.W., Alström, P., Davidson, P., Evans, T.D., Poole, C.M., Tan Setha and Timmins, R.J. (2001) A new species of wagtail from the lower Mekong basin. *Bull. British Ornithologists' Club* 121(3): 152-182.

127 Daconto, G. (ed.) (2001) *Environmental Protection and Community Development in Siphandone Wetland Project*. CESVI, Bergamo, Italy.

128 Saint Girons, H. (1972). Les serpents du Cambodge. *Mémoires du Muséum National d'Histoire Naturelle. Série A, Zoologie, Paris*.

129 Rainboth, W. J. (1996) as 9 above.

130 Poulsen, A. (2003) Migrating masses. *Catch and Culture* 9 (2): 10-11.

131 Roule, M. Louis (1916) Description de l'Hippocamus aimei sp. nov., espece nouvelle d'eau douce, provenant du Mekong. *Bull. Mus. Nat. Hist. Paris* 22: 11-13.

132 Roberts T. (2002) Payanak as a mythical animal and as the living species Regalecus glesne (Oarfish, Regalecidae, Lampridiformes). *Natural History Bulletin of the Siam Society*. 50: 211-224.

133 Seng Kim Hout, Pech Bunnat, Poole, C.M., Tordoff, A.W., Davidson, P. and Delattre, E. (2003) *Directory of Important Bird Areas in Cambodia: key sites for conservation*. DFW, DNCP, BirdLife International and WCS Cambodia Program, Phnom Penh.

134 Fisheries Office, Ratanakiri Province. (2000) *A study of the downstream impacts of the Yali Dam in the Sesan River Basin in Ratanakiri Province, Northeast Cambodia*. Report prepared in cooperation with the Non-Timber Forest Products (NTFP) Project, Ratanakiri Province, Cambodia.

135 Claassen, A.H. (2003) *Abundance, distribution, and reproductive success of sandbar nesting birds Below a hydropower dam on the Sesan River, northeastern Cambodia*. WWF, WCS and BirdLife International. Phnom Penh.

136 Dore, J and Yu Xiaogang (2004) *Yunnan Hydropower Expansion: Update on China's energy industry reforms and the Nu, Lancang and Jinsha hydropower dams*. Working Paper from Chiang Mai University's Unit for Social and Environmental Research, and Green Watershed.

137 Starr, P. (2004) Low water blues. *Catch and Culture* 10(1): 4-6.

138 Piyaporn Wongruang and Tul Pinkaew (2004) Mekong commission downplays impact of Chinese dams. *Bangkok Post* 20 November 2004.

139 Pearce, F. (2004) Chinese dams blamed for Mekong's bizarre flow. 25 March 2004. *New Scientist*. www.newscientist.com.

140 Roberts, T. (2001) Killing the Mekong: China's fluvicidal hydropower- cum-navigation development scheme. *Natural History Bulletin of the Siam Society* 49: 143-159.

141 Osborne, M. (2004) River at risk: the Mekong and the water politics of China and Southeast Asia. Lowy Institute Paper 02. Double Bay, Australia.

142 Roberts, T. (2001) as 140 above.

143 Osborne, M. (2004) as 141 above.

144 Wain, B. (2004) Beijing's clumsy manoeuvres. *Far Eastern Economic Review* August 26, 2004. www.feer.com

145 Osborne, M. (2004) as 141 above.

146 Yardley, J. (2004) Beijing suspends plan for large dam. *International Herald Tribune* April 8, 2004.

147 Yangtze at Limit of Energy Exploitation. *China Daily* April 1, 2005. http://www.china.org.cn/english/2005/Apr/124454.htm

148 International Institute for Energy Conservation http://www.iiec.org/

149 Bou Saroeun (1999) Amid the destruction, local initiatives bring hope for the environment. *Phnom Penh Post* June 11 - 24, 1999.

150 Beasley, I. (2004) *Mekong River Irrawaddy dolphin conservation and management plan 2004-2008*. Department of Fisheries and Mekong Dolphin Conservation Project. Phnom Penh.

# VISITING SITES MENTIONED IN THIS BOOK

## PHNOM KULEN – MOUNTAIN AND FOREST

**Phnom Kulen and Kbal Spean, Siem Reap**
Both are easily accessible by car from Siem Reap and any tour guide can arrange visits.

**Seima Biodiversity Conservation Area, Mondulkiri**
The Forestry Administration with support from WCS manages the conservation project from the former logging camp at Labake along Road #76 to Sen Monorom, Mondulkiri. The area is not set up for visitors, but adventurous travelers can enquire at the WCS office in Phnom Penh. WCS, #21, St.21, Sangkat Tonle Bassac, Phnom Penh. Tel: 023 217 295.
E-mail: Cambodia@wcs.org.
For more information: http://www.wcs.org/international/Asia/Cambodia/seimabiodiversity

## ANGKOR – THE ANCIENT ENVIRONMENT

**Birdwatching at Angkor**
The best temple for birdwatching in the Angkor complex is Preah Khan which has the best forest and a number of the rarer species such as Alexandrine Parakeet.
Other good birdwatching options include:
• Walking the walls of Angkor Thom, from which you can look directly into the upper and middle storey of the trees.
• The north-eastern section of the Angkor Wat moat which is excellent for waterbirds, particularly for ducks in the dry season.
*A Birdwatcher's Guide to Angkor* supplement to Cambodia Bird News #5 is essential reading.

**Chhep and Tmatboey, Preah Vihear**
In remote Preah Vihear, WCS works with the Government on a project to promote conservation through tourism, by using ibises and vultures as 'flagship' species. Local communities have an agreement not to hunt endangered bird species in exchange for tourist visits. Visiting groups contribute to community development by staying in villagers' houses and employing local guides. If groups are successful they are asked to make a donation to a 'village

conservation fund'. The fund is used to pay for community development.
A vulture restaurant is maintained in Chhep District, about 6 hours drive to the east of Tbeng Meanchey, the provincial town of Preah Vihear. Access is only possible by 4WD and is limited to the months of December-April. A camp for field staff is maintained about 1km from the feeding station. A complete restaurant takes 5-6 days, from killing the cow to when the vultures leave the area, with peak numbers seen on days 2-4. If a restaurant is requested at least one week before, it can then be timed so that peak vulture numbers can be seen. The cost is $200, including the cost of the cow, maintaining hides, and field rangers. It does not include transport, accommodation, food, or the accompanying tourist guide.
A similar scheme is run for tourists to see the very rare Giant and White-shouldered Ibises at the village of Tmatboey about 1 hours drive to the west of Tbeng Meanchey. Again access is easiest by 4WD during the dry season in November-May, however, the village is accessible and both ibises can be seen year round. Independent travelers can organize this directly with WCS (contact details as Chapter 1 above)
E-mail: wcs.ibis@everyday.com.kh
Alternatively tours can be arranged in Phnom Penh through Monsoon Tours: http://www.monsoon-tours.com. #15, St.105, Phnom Penh. Tel/Fax: 023 211 190.
E-mail: contact@monsoon-tours.com
monsoontours@online.com.kh
http://www.monsoon-tours.com/WCS_NW_Tourism_Info.pdf
Or in Siem Reap by Terre Cambodge (contact details as Chapter 4 below).
For more information: http://www.wcs.org/international/Asia/Cambodia/NorthernPlain.

## PHNOM KRAOM AND THE FLOODPLAIN

**Phnom Kraom, Siem Reap**
On the road to Chong Kneas, this hill is easily accessible by car or motorbike from Siem Reap. There is a road to the top where there is a temple and an excellent view of the lake and floodplain in any season.

### Krous Kraom, Kompong Thom

Located 10-15 km south-west from Kompong Thom town Krous Kraom is about 120 km² in extent. It is accessible only in the dry season by motorbike or 4WD and the journey takes around an hour from Kompong Thom town. Leave Kompong Thom on Road #6 to Phnom Penh and after 6 km turn right onto a good laterite road leading to the village of Roulos. Continue south through the village and follow the main oxcart track south for another 5-6 km, after which you'll be entering a mix of agriculture and scrub where floricans are found. Take plenty of water as it gets very hot and there's no shade.

### Stung, Kompong Thom

As the area around Krous Kraom is increasingly being converted to recession rice agriculture, the grasslands of Stung although further distant maybe a better option. They are located about half way between Kompong Thom and Siem Reap, with the journey taking about an hour along the road from each followed by a 30 minute drive into the grasslands (15 km) from Stung town. The turn-off is only 30 minutes south of the junction with the road to Koh Ker temple and Preah Vihear.

### Ang Trapeang Thmor, Banteay Meanchey

Accessible by car from Siem Reap along Road #6 towards Sisophon. After about 60 km turn north at a cross-roads called Prey Mwan. Landmarks at the turnoff include a florican sign! Drive 15 km to reach Phnom Srok, where you turn left at the roundabout and continue for another 7–8 km. The road passes through several villages, after passing a pagoda, turn left to reach the reservoir. The government conservation team office is along the village track about a hundred meters before the pagoda and staff can assist with guiding etc.
*Birdwatching in Cambodia - Ang Tropeang Thmor Sarus Crane Reserve* in Cambodia Bird News #12 is essential reading.

## CHONG KNEAS AND PREK TOAL – LIVING ON THE LAKE

### Chong Kneas, Siem Reap

Easily accessible from Siem Reap through any tour guide. Insist that you stop at the GECKO environment centre http://jinja.apsara.org/gecko/gecko.htm and refuse to stop at captive any floating houses or restaurants displaying wildlife such as pelicans and storks.

### Prek Toal, Battambang

The floating village is accessible from Chong Kneas by chartering your own boat directly, taking the daily speedboat ferry to Battambang and alighting in Prek Toal or taking the daily local boat to Prek Toal. Once you reach the village, ask to be taken to the Environment Centre where there are rooms for rent for staying overnight and meals can be ordered.

### Kompong Phluk and Kompong Khleang, Siem Reap

About 25-30km southeast of Siem Reap town, both are accessible by car and boat depending on the season and visits can be arranged by tour guides in Siem Reap.

### Chnouk Tru, Kompong Chhnang and Kompong Luong, Pursat

The former is accessible by boat from the town of Kompong Chhnang, the latter by boat or road, depending on the season, from Road #5 between Kompong Chhnang and Pursat.

Terre Cambodge www.terrecambodge.com near Psa Cha in Siem Reap can organize boat trips to any of the above villages. Tel: 012 843 401. Fax. 063 964 391. E-mail: info@terrecambodge.com

### Central Cardamoms, Koh Kong

Access is currently difficult, but adventurous tourists can potentially arrange visits to the Siamese Crocodile sites in the Areng Valley or Veal Veng by enquiring at the Phnom Penh offices of Conservation International, #29, St.294, Phnom Penh, Tel. 023 214 627.
or Fauna and Flora International, #8b St.398, Phnom Penh, Cambodia. Tel./Fax: 023 211 142.
E-mail: fficambodia@everyday.com.kh

## THE FISHING LOTS OF BATTAMBANG

### Chong Kneas, Prek Toal and floating villages

Accessible as above. Crocodiles can be seen in floating cages behind many of the houses, ask at the Environment Centre.

## Psa Kraom, Siem Reap

This market, to the south of Siem Reap town, little visited by tourists, is where – in season – sells most of the watersnakes and fish for local consumption unloaded at Chong Kneas. Any taxi driver in Siem Reap can guide you there.

## Tonle Sap Exhibition, Siem Reap

Krousar Thmey, a Cambodian Foundation assisting deprived children, has an excellent permanent exhibition about the Tonle Sap which is free to enter. As you leave Siem Reap on the road leading to Angkor Wat it is the right side. Any taxi driver can take you there. http://www.myfriend.org/krousar-thmey/tonlesape

## PREK TOAL - THE CORE AREAS OF THE BIOSPHERE RESERVE

### Prek Toal Core Area

Accessible as above. Once at the Environment Centre, staff can arrange permit and boat rental to access the Core Area. Rates are set and are posted on the wall. Alternatively a day's guided tour can be arranged direct from Siem Reap with Osmose, a local ecotourism initiative located at the Sam Veasna Centre in Siem Reap. http://www.osmosetonlesap.org
Tel: 012 832 812.
E-mail: osmose@online.com.kh
For more information: http://www.wcs.org/international/Asia/Cambodia/Tonle_Sap
*A Birdwatcher's Guide to the Tonle Sap Great Lake* supplement to Cambodia Bird News #7 is essential reading.

### Beong Chhma and Stung Sen Core Area, Siem Reap and Kompong Thom

Both are difficult to access without guides. Enquire in Siem Reap at Osmose or the Sam Veasna Centre (Near Wat Bo, just past the Angkor Village Hotel). Terre Cambodge in Siem Reap (contact detail as above) can also organize trips to these areas.

### Sre Ambel

The town of Sre Ambel is found by taking Road #48 turning right off Road #4 two hours drive from Phnom Penh. Local speedboats can be rented to travel upriver or to visit the mangroves downriver.

## THE TONLE SAP RIVER AND PHNOM PENH

### Phnom Penh Riverfront

Caged birds are for sale daily at Preah Ang Dongkar in front of the Royal Palace.

The Water Festival takes place in early November and boats race along the Tonle Sap directly in front of Phnom Penh.

During the winter large numbers of Whiskered Terns and other waterbirds can be see flying and feeding along the river. Tourist boats can be hired on the riverfront to travel downriver towards Kien Svay for the best birdwatching.

### Tonle Sap River dai fishery, Kandal and Kompong Chhnang

At the peak of the fishing season in early January the fishing dais and large amounts of activity can be seen between the river and Road #5 north from Phnom Penh towards Kompong Chhnang.

### Wat Phnom, Phnom Penh

Phnom Penh's sole remaining colony of flying-foxes occupy the trees of the Cambodian Government (CDC) offices directly north-east of Wat Phnom. Prayer release birds are for sale along the roadside most days and groups of Long-tailed Macaques harass visitors around the temple.

### Basset Marshes, Kandal

This is the best birdwatching area easily accessible from Phnom Penh. Take the Road #5 north from Phnom Penh and after 12km turn left at Prek Phneou onto the Kop Srou flood control dyke and the wetland is soon visible on your left.
*Birdwatching in Cambodia Wetlands of the Four-Arm Plain* in Cambodia Bird News #10 and *Birding at the Basset Marshes – an update* in Cambodia Bird News #11 are essential reading.

### Koh Thom, Kandal

Wat Kompong Kor (well known for it is also the location of the Cambodia Vipassana Centre), is on the island of Koh Thom in the Bassac River. It is accessible by road south from Takhmau along Road #21, west of the river, for 35km and then by local ferry.

**Kompi and Sambor, Kratie**

The village of Kompi is a 15 km taxi or moto ride north of the town of Kratie along Road #7. A large dolphin statue and a sign clearly mark the entrance. Tourism is managed by the local authorities and visitors must purchase tickets at the site to be taken out in a local boat to see the dolphins. Although they are most concentrated in the dry season, animals can be seen here throughout the year. For those more adventurous who want to continue upriver, the stretch between Kompi and the next river town of Sambor is excellent for many riverine birds including the endemic Mekong Wagtail. For more information on the dolphin watching check out http://www.mekongdolphin.org

Alternatively tours can be arranged from Phnom Penh by Monsoon Tours (contact details as above) http://www.mekong-dolphin.com/entrance.htm

**Sesan River, Ratanakiri**

The best time to visit the Sesan is between mid-February and mid-May. To look for the Black-bellied Terns take a boat downstream for 2-3 hours from the town of Veunsai towards Phum Voen Hoy. If this is organised with the staff of Virachey National Park the boat driver may even be familiar with the birds and the site. If not the birds can be found around Koh Romleung, about 1.5-2km downriver from the village of Phum Voen Hoy. This island also has a selection of other key species, including River Terns, River Lapwings and Great Thick-knees.

**Boeng Prek Lapeou, Takeo**

In the wet season accessible by speedboat from the town of Takeo. In the dry season take Road #2 south from Takeo town towards Vietnam and then turn left towards the village of Koh Andeh. For more information contact the office of BirdLife International in Phnom Penh.
#25B, St.294, Phnom Penh. Tel/Fax: 023 993 631.
E-mail: birdlife@online.com.kh

# FURTHER READING

**Field Guides - Birds**
Robson, C. (2001) *Birds of Southeast Asia*. New Holland, London.

**Field Guides - Fish**
Rainboth, W. J. (1996) *Fishes of the Cambodian Mekong*. FAO, Rome

**Field Guides - Mammals**
Francis, C.M. (2001) *A photographic guide to the mammals of South-east Asia*. New Holland, London.
Parr, J.W.K. (2003) *A guide to the large mammals of Thailand*. Sarakadee. Bangkok

**Field Guides - Reptiles**
Cox, M. J., van Dijk, P. P., Nabhitabhata, J. and Thirakhupt, K. (1998) *A photographic guide to snakes and other reptiles of Thailand and South-east Asia*. Asia Books, Bangkok.
Stuart, B. L., van Dijk, P. P., and Hendrie, D. B. (2002) *Photographic guide to the turtles of Thailand, Laos, Vietnam and Cambodia*. Wildlife Conservation Society, Phnom Penh.

**Angkor**
Michael F. and Jacques, C. (2004) *Angkor – Cities & Temples*. River Books, Bangkok.
Roveda, V. (2005) *Images of the Gods – Khmer Mythology in Cambodia, Laos & Thailand*. River Books, Bangkok.
Mouhot, H. (2000) *Travels in Siam, Cambodia, Laos, and Annam*, White Lotus. Bangkok.
Coe, M. (2003) *Angkor and the Khmer civilization*. Thames and Hudson, London.
Higham, C. (2003) *The civilization of Angkor*. Phoenix, London.

**The Mekong**
Garnier, F. (1996) *Travels in Cambodia and part of Laos. The Mekong Exploration Commission Report (1866-1868) – Volume 1*. White Lotus, Bangkok.
Osborne, M. E. (2000) *The Mekong, turbulent past, uncertain future*. Allen and Unwin, St Leonards, Australia.

Osborne, M. E. (2004) *River at risk: the Mekong and the water politics of China and Southeast Asia*. Lowy Institute Paper 02. Double Bay, Australia.
http://www.lowyinstitute.org/

## MAGAZINES AND JOURNALS

**Cambodia Bird News**
Twice yearly magazine produced in both Cambodian and English. It is essential reading for anybody interested in birds and wildlife in Cambodia. Available by subscription from WCS, PO Box 1620, Phnom Penh, Cambodia. Cambodia@wcs.org

**Birding Asia**
Twice yearly magazine of the Oriental Bird Club, which along with the annual journal Forktail regularly includes articles and information related to Cambodia birds.
www.orientalbirdclub.org

**Natural History Bulletin of the Siam Society**
Regional scientific journal published annually by the Siam Society, regularly containing articles of relevance to Cambodia.
www.siam-society.org

## WEB SITES

**APSARA**
http://www.autoritcapsara.org
The website of the Cambodian Government authority responsible for managing Angkor.

**Cambodian Ministry of Agriculture, Forestry and Fisheries**
http://www.maff.gov.kh
An excellent website with links to the Forestry Administration and Department of Fisheries and various resources and statistics.

**Cambodian Ministry of Environment**
http://www.moe.gov.kh

**Center for Khmer Studies**

http://www.khmerstudies.org

Based In Wat Damnak, Siem Reap, the CKS website includes a good searchable online library of Khmer material.

**Directory of Important Bird Areas in Cambodia**

http://www.birdlifeindochina.org/iba_cambodia/indexE.htm

The full IBA directory and maps in both English and Cambodian.

**Fisheries Action Coalition Team**

http://www.fact.org.kh/english/english.htm

An NGO coalition working on fisheries issues around the Tonle Sap. The web site includes their downloadable *Tonle Sap Watch Newsletter*.

**GECKO Center**

http://jinja.apsara.org/gecko/gecko.htm

Floating environment centre in Chong Kneas run by the provincial environment authorities with support from FAO.

**International Rivers Network**

http://www.irn.org/programs/mekong

International NGO that campaigns against dam schemes worldwide.

**Mekong Dolphin Conservation Project**

http://www.mekongdolphin.org

**Mekonginfo**

http://www.mekonginfo.org

Hosts the website for the Tonle Sap Biosphere Reserve site and an excellent online library resource.

**Mekong River Commission**

http://www.mrcmekong.org

Including the excellent fisheries newsletter *Catch and Culture*, and many downloadable MRC publications and resources.

**Osmose**

http://www.osmosetonlesap.org

Ecotourism initiaitive supporting local environmental education and development initiatives on the Tonle Sap, primarily in Prek Toal.

**Southeast Asia Rivers Network**

http://www.searin.org/mekong_en.htm

Good regional resource on Mekong issues, particularly the river-blasting.

**Tonle Sap Modelling Project**

http://www.eia.fi/wup-fin and
http://www.water.hut.fi/~mkummu

Several downloadable technical reports and papers on the Tonle Sap.

**Wildlife Conservation Society**

http://www.wcs.org/international/Asia/Cambodia

Descriptions of WCS projects in Cambodia.

**World Monument Fund**

http://www.wmf.org/html/programs/angkor.html

WMF support the renovation of Preah Khan, one of the most important temples in the Angkor complex. The website outlines their work with some excellent links.

# ACKNOWLEDGEMENTS

Without two people I would never have embarked upon this project or seen it through to the end. Firstly, Eleanor Briggs, a great friend with whom I have worked for many years in Cambodia, and without whose wonderful photographs and regular support and encouragement this would not have been possible. Secondly, my publisher and longtime friend Narisa Chakrabongse, whom I first met when we were students together at the University of London's School of Oriental and African Studies. Without our shared interests in the environment of Southeast Asia, and the faith and patience of her and her colleague Paisarn Piemmettawat at River Books, this would never have happened.

For their personal support to me and their help to the Wildlife Conservation Society (WCS) throughout my time in Cambodia I would like to thank the following members of the Royal Cambodian Government: H. E. Mok Mareth, Minister of Environment (MoE); H. E. Chan Sarun, Minister of Agriculture, Forestry and Fisheries; H. E. Ty Sokhun, Director of the Forest Administration (FA); H. E. Nao Thouk, Director of the Fisheries Department; H. E. Vann Sophanna, Director of the FA Northern Region; Chay Samith, Director of the Department of Nature Conservation and Protection, MoE; and Men Phymean, Director of the Wildlife Protection Office, FA.

I would similarly like to thank my bosses at WCS, John Robinson and Joshua Ginsberg for their continued support.

Over eight years in Cambodia I have had conversations with many people that have helped me to understand just a little more about the country and its issues. The thoughts and ideas of all the people below are in some way reflected in this book, many will not realize that they have helped me, but I thank you all. I hope I have given everybody due credit, but if I've overlooked anybody or misrepresented anything, the mistake is mine alone and I apologise.

An Dara, David Ashwell, Ian Baird, Isabel Beasley, Steve Bridges, Gavin Bourchier, Kevin Callinan, Ian Campbell, David Catling, Chea Vannaren, Tom Clements, James Compton, Pete Davidson, Deap Loeung, Peter Degen, Etienne Delattre, Will Duckworth, Tom Evans, Roland Fletcher, Eva Galabru, Wim Giesen, Martin Gilbert, Frédéric Goes, James Goodman, Rick Gregory, Wayne Gum, Hans Guttman, Heng Sovannara, Zeb Hogan, Rohan Holloway, Hong Chamnan, Ross Hughes, Paul Im, Keo Omaliss, Kong Kim Sreng, Matti Kummu, Tom Kunneke, Lay Khim, Long Kheng, Andrew McDonald, Bruce McKenney, Mark Mallalieu, Mao Kosal, Andy Maxwell, Richard Melville, Men Soriyun, Meng Monyrak, Vicki Nelson, Neo Bonheur, Harry Nesbitt, Net Neath, Nathalie Nivot-Goes, Ted Osius, Mike Ounsted, Pech Sokhem, Phay Somany, Steve Platt, Tyson Roberts, Philip Round, Philip Rundel, John Sanday, Seng Kim Hout, Seng Teak, Bryan Stuart, Philip Stott, Rena Sugita, Sun Hean, Sun Visal, Suon Phalla, Tan Setha, John Thorbjarnarson, Rob Timmins, Rob Tizard, Tran Triet, Joe Walston, Dave Ware, Yi Thon and Niek van Zalinge.

Finally none of this would have been possible without the support and understanding of my family: Siny, Tola, Sreyneath and Michael from whom I have learnt more about Cambodia than anybody.

*Colin Poole*

First, I would like to thank Colin Poole who has been a great friend and partner in several projects involving my photographs. He has also given me many opportunities to work throughout the country and, with his wife, Siny and their wonderful family, has made me feel totally at home in Cambodia. Without his insightful writings, this book would not have been possible.

Next, I thank George Archibald and the International Crane Foundation for bringing me back to Cambodia in 1991 for the first aerial survey perhaps ever and for making possible the work in Prek Toal to stop the collection of eggs and chicks from what turned out to be the largest waterbird colony in Southeast Asia. Chhim Somean offered support as well. Many thanks to H. E. Dr. Mok Mareth, Minister of Environment, who first suggested the presence of cranes near the Tonle Sap and to H. E. Nao Thuok, Director of the Fisheries Department, who took me out onto the lake for the first time and showed me stork chicks being raised for the New Year's feast on the porch of every floating house. His support and wise council were indispensable during the 1997 waterbird protection project. Bernard O'Callaghan offered a base in Phnom Penh and Sun Hean skillful direction for our project as I worked and photographed with Haidy Ear-Dupuy, a conservation biology graduate student critical to the project because of her training and fine language skills. Our counterparts, Keo Omaliss and Hong Chamnan were important team members and Pol Chhea the owner of Battambang fishing lot #2 let us enter the forest and the bird colonies and supported our work. Frederic Goes and Sun Visal have created an impressive project from those beginnings.

Since 1997, I have been fortunate to travel widely with Hong Chamnan both to photograph wildlife projects throughout the country for the Wildlife Conservation Society and to visit some of Cambodia's remote archaeological treasures. It is to him that I owe my smooth travels and deep appreciation of his country and its people. And to WCS that I owe the opportunity to do so much work here.

For their support and guidance, I would like to thank H. E. Chan Sarun, Minister of Agriculture, Fisheries and Forestry and H. E. Ty Sokhun, Director of Forest Administration. Thanks also to H. E. Vann Sophanna for advice and connections during work to create the Ang Trapeang Thmor Sarus Crane Reserve of which the late Sam Veasna was the major inspiration. It was an honor to work with him on this important project.

Joe Walston, Natalie Nivot and Keo Yada have given invaluable help and encouragement over the years. Heng Sovannara showed me his turtle project in Sre Ambel. Phay Somany took me to his dolphin project in Kratie and to the *dai* fisheries on the Tonle Sap river. Martin Gilbert invited me to his vulture restaurant in Preah Vihear. An Dara visited the fruitbat colony in Koh Thom with me. Pete Davidson invited me on his Giant Ibis census in Preah Vihear. Men Soriyun took me to Mondulkiri to photograph his team at work in Keo Seima. I walked with Phet Phaktra into Phnong villages. Kérya Chau Sun of APSARA kindly organized the authority for me to photograph within the Angkor Park. My time in Cambodia has been a glorious experience which has enriched my life immeasurably. Last and most importantly I must thank all the patient and kind Cambodians whose names I do not know. They so generously helped me to make photographs of them and their country.

*Eleanor Briggs*

# INDEX